No Bad Kids

Toddler Discipline Without Shame

Janet Lansbury

Janet Lansbury

No Bad Kids: Toddler Discipline Without Shame
Copyright (c) 2014 by Janet Lansbury

ISBN: 978-1499351118

Published by JLML Press, 2014

For permission requests, please email the publisher, subject line: "Elevating Child Care Permissions" at MBLansbury@gmail.com

Identifying details, including names, have been changed except by permission and for those pertaining to the author's family members. With exceptions, material contained in this book is available on the author's website. This book is not intended as a substitute for advice from a licensed professional.

~

Cover Photo and Design: Sara Prince
www.bonzochoochmushyandme.com

For more information about the author, please visit her website at: **www.JanetLansbury.com.**

Table of Contents

Forward

When it comes to discipline, parents are faced with a deluge of disparate expert advice that can be perplexing, contradictory, and sometimes just plain impossible to follow. Should parents spank, bribe, reward, ignore, give consequences, or order a time-out? Does gentle discipline mean letting children rule the roost? Should parents use threats, distractions, games, charts, timers, count to three, or perfect "that look"?

It's no wonder so many parents are confused, frustrated, and paralyzed. It's no wonder they find themselves losing their confidence, and often their tempers.

It doesn't have to be that way.

Unlike the majority of prominent child development advisers on discipline, I've spent years in parent/toddler classrooms putting theory into practice. I've witnessed (a thousand times over) the kinds of interventions and responses that actually work, as well as the ones that never work, and the ones that might work once or twice but ultimately create even bigger power struggles or undermine trust between kids and their parents.

Toddlers, especially, are prone to pushing limits. It is their job as active learners and explorers and developmentally appropriate. It is a natural expression of their intense mix of emotions as they struggle to become more autonomous. Successful guidance provides children the safety and comfort they need to flourish. When boundaries work, children don't need to test them as often. They trust their parents and caregivers; therefore, their world. They feel freer and calmer and can focus on the important things: play, learning, socializing, and being happy-go-lucky kids.

When setting limits, the emotional state of the parent almost always dictates the child's reaction. If we lack clarity and confidence, lose our temper or are unsure, tense, frazzled, or frustrated — this will unsettle our kids and very likely lead to more undesirable behavior. We are gods in our children's eyes, and our feelings always set the tone. With this understanding, it's easy to see why struggles with discipline can become a discouragingly vicious cycle.

As the title of this book states, in my world there are no bad kids, just impressionable, conflicted young people wrestling with emotions and impulses, trying to communicate their feelings and needs the only way they know how. When we characterize them as *bad* because we're frustrated, confused, or offended by their behavior, we are doing them a great disservice. It is a negative label, a source of shame they may eventually start to believe about themselves.

My parenting philosophy and my perception of children and our relationships with them are all informed by the teachings of my friend and mentor, child specialist Magda Gerber. Through Magda and the organization she founded, RIE (Resources for Infant Educarers), I gained clarity as a mother and developed the respectful, fulfilling, *effective* approach to parenting that I've shared with millions of others as a teacher and writer.

At the core of RIE Parenting is a radical concept:

Babies are whole people – sentient, aware, intuitive and communicative. They are natural learners, explorers, and scientists able to test hypotheses, solve problems, and understand language and abstract ideas.

Not what one would consider conventional parenting wisdom, but clinical and scientific findings and published research* have confirmed these amazing infant abilities that Magda Gerber recognized 50 years ago.

Yet all too often we are still treating our infants and toddlers as if they are vacant, unaware, and incapable of understanding or communicating with us. Conversely, we might expect our children to be able to handle adult situations (like an afternoon shopping excursion at the mall) with a level of maturity and emotional self-control they have not yet developed. These inaccurate perceptions can lead parents in an unproductive direction, especially in regard to discipline issues.

Ultimately, the big secret to successful discipline is ditching the quick-fix tricks, gimmicks, and all other manipulative tactics and simply being honest with our babies and toddlers (What a concept!). This is the most basic level of respect RIE teaches, and embracing it is as liberating as it sounds.

This book is a collection of my articles pertaining to common toddler behaviors and how respectful parenting practices can be applied to benefit both parents and children. It covers such common topics as punishment, cooperation, boundaries, testing, tantrums, hitting, and more.

I am privileged to receive a steady stream of letters from parents with questions and concerns about discipline. Loving, thoughtful parents simply want to know how to give their kids healthy limits and gain their cooperation. Many are at their wits' end and desperate for answers.

Other letters, which are usually the highlight of my day, are personal success stories describing a toddler dilemma and how the parent addressed it by putting respectful care principles into action. I have included several of these letters in this collection, along with my responses, because they are illuminating, relatable, and encouraging.

My hope is that this book will serve as a practical tool for parents who are anticipating or experiencing those critical years when toddlers are developmentally obliged to test the limits of our patience and love. Armed with knowledge and a better sense of the world through our children's eyes, this period of uncertainty can afford a myriad of opportunities to forge unbreakable bonds of trust, respect, and love.

*Gopnik, Alison. (July, 2010). How Babies Think. *Scientific American*, 76-81

1.

No Bad Kids
Toddler Discipline Without Shame

A toddler acting out is not shameful, nor is it behavior that needs punishing. It's a cry for attention, a shout-out for sleep, or a call to action for firmer, more consistent limits. It is the push-pull of your toddler testing his burgeoning independence. He has the overwhelming impulse to step out of bounds, while also desperately needing to know he is securely reined in.

There is no question that children need discipline. As Magda Gerber said: "Lack of discipline is not kindness, it is neglect." The key to healthy and effective discipline is our attitude.

Toddlerhood is the perfect time to hone parenting skills that will provide the honest, direct, and compassionate leadership our children will depend on for years to come. Here are some guidelines:

1. Begin with a predictable environment and realistic expectations. A predictable daily routine enables a baby to anticipate what is expected of him. That is the beginning of discipline. Home is the ideal place for infants and toddlers to spend the majority of their day. Of course, we must take them with us to do errands sometimes, but we cannot expect a toddler's best behavior at dinner parties, long afternoons at the mall, or when his days are loaded with scheduled activities.

2. Don't be afraid or take misbehavior personally. When toddlers act out in my classes, the parents often worry that their child might be a brat, a bully, an aggressive kid. When parents project those fears, it can cause the child to internalize the negative personas, or at least pick up on the parent's tension, which often exacerbates the misbehavior.

Instead of labeling a child's action, learn to nip the behavior in the bud by disallowing it nonchalantly. If your child throws a ball at your face, try not to get annoyed. He doesn't do it because he dislikes you, and he's not a bad child. He is asking you (toddler-style) for the limits that he needs and may not be getting.

3. Respond in the moment, calmly, like a CEO. Finding the right tone for setting limits can take a bit of practice. Lately, I've been encouraging parents that struggle with this to imagine they are a successful CEO and that their toddler is a respected underling. The CEO guides and leads others with confident efficiency. She doesn't use an unsure, questioning tone, get angry or emotional. Our child needs to feel that we are not nervous about his behavior or ambivalent about establishing rules. He finds comfort when we are effortlessly in charge.

Lectures, emotional reactions, scolding, and punishments do not give our toddler the clarity he needs and can create guilt and shame. A simple, matter-of-fact, "I won't let you do that. If you throw that again I will need to take it away," while blocking the behavior with our hands, is the best response. But react immediately. Once the moment has passed, it is too late. Wait for the next one!

4. Speak in first person. Parents often get in the habit of calling themselves "Mommy" or "Daddy". Toddlerhood is the time to change over into first person for the most honest, direct communication possible. Toddlers test boundaries to clarify the rules. When I say, "Mommy doesn't want Emma to hit the dog," I'm not giving my child the direct ('you' and 'me') interaction she needs.

5. No time-out. I always think of Magda asking in her grandmotherly Hungarian accent, "Time out of what? Time out of life?" Magda was a believer in straightforward, honest language between a parent and child. She didn't believe in gimmicks like time-out, especially to control a child's behavior or punish him.

If a child misbehaves in a public situation, the child is usually indicating he's tired, losing control, and needs to leave. Carrying a child to the car to go home, even if he kicks and screams, is the sensitive and respectful way to handle the issue. Sometimes a child has a tantrum at home and needs to be taken to his room to flail and cry in our presence until he regains self-control. These are not punishments, but caring responses.

6. Consequences. A toddler learns discipline best when he experiences natural consequences for his behavior, rather than a disconnected punishment like time-out. If a child throws food, his mealtime is over. If a child refuses to get dressed, we won't be able to go to the park today. These parental responses appeal to a child's sense of fairness. The child may still react negatively to the consequence, but he does not feel manipulated or shamed.

7. Don't discipline a child for crying. Children need rules for behavior, but their emotional responses to the limits we set (or to anything else, for that matter) should be allowed, even encouraged. Toddlerhood can be a time of intense, conflicting feelings. Children may need to express anger, frustration, confusion, exhaustion, and disappointment, especially if they don't get what they want because we've set a limit. A child needs the freedom to safely express his feelings without our judgment. He may need a pillow to punch. Give him one.

8. Unconditional love. Withdrawing our affection as a form of discipline teaches a child that our love and support turns on a dime, evaporating because of his momentary misbehavior. How can that foster a sense of security? Alfie Kohn's *New York Times* article, "When A Parent's 'I Love You' Means 'Do As I Say'," explores the damage this kind of conditional parenting causes, as the child grows to resent, distrust, and dislike his parents, feel guilt, shame, and a lack of self-worth.

9. Spanking – NEVER. Most damaging of all to a relationship of trust are spankings. And spanking is a predictor of violent behavior. A *Time Magazine* article by Alice Park ("The Long-Term Effects of Spanking") reports findings from a recent study which point to "the strongest evidence yet that children's short-term response to spanking may make them act out more in the long run. Of the nearly 2,500 youngsters in the study, those who were spanked more frequently at age 3 were much more likely to be aggressive by age 5."

Purposely inflicting pain on a child cannot be done with love. Sadly, however, the child often learns to associate the two.

Loving our child does not mean keeping him happy all the time and avoiding power struggles. Often it is doing what feels hardest for us to do: saying "no" and meaning it.

Our children deserve our direct, honest responses so they can internalize right and wrong and develop the authentic self-discipline needed to respect and be respected by others. As Magda wrote in *Dear Parent: Caring for Infants With Respect*, "The goal is inner-discipline, self-confidence and joy in the act of cooperation."

2.

Why Toddlers Push Limits

Limit-pushing behavior can confound even the most attuned parent or caregiver. Why would our sweet darling throw her toy at us when we've *just* asked her not to, and then add insult to injury by smirking? Is she evil? Does she have a pressing need to practice throwing skills? Maybe she just hates us...

Sensitive, intensely emotional, and severely lacking in impulse control, toddlers often have unusual ways of expressing their needs and feelings. If it's any consolation, these behaviors don't make sense to our children either. The simple explanation is the unfortunate combination of an immature prefrontal cortex and the turbulent emotions of toddlerhood. More simply: children are easily overwhelmed by impulses bigger and stronger than they are.

In other words, your child very likely understood that you didn't want her to hit you, her friends, siblings, and pets; dump her food or water onto the floor; whine, scream, and call you "stupid"; but her impulses made a different choice. And though she smirks, this isn't out of ill will.

Rule #1: *Never, ever take a child's limit-pushing behavior personally.*

Our children love, appreciate, and need us more than they can ever say. Remind yourself of these truths multiple times daily until you've internalized them, because a healthy perspective on limit-pushing is a crucial starting point.

Respecting children means understanding their stage of development, not reacting to their age-appropriate behavior as if they are our peers.

Here are the most common reasons young children push limits:

1. SOS! I can't function. Young children seem to be the last people on earth to register their own fatigue or hunger. They seem programmed to push on, and sometimes their bodies will take possession of their minds and transmit SOS messages to us through attention-getting behavior.

When I think about my own children's limit-pushing behavior, the examples that immediately come to mind are about fatigue:

There was the day at RIE class when my toddler son (who has always seemed to have social savvy) suddenly started hitting and pushing. *Ah-ha. He's tired and has had enough of this.* I let him know I heard him and that we'd be leaving: "I don't want you to hit. I think you're letting me know you're tired and ready to go home, right?"

But then I got involved in a discussion with one of the other parents and forgot for a moment and, no surprise, he hit again. Oops. Totally my fault. "Sorry, B, I told you we would leave and then started talking. Thanks for reminding me we need to go."

Then there was the family trip when one of my

daughters, age four at the time, uncharacteristically spoke rudely to my mother. Taken aback for a moment (How could she?) but determined to remain calm, I intervened: "I can't let you talk to Grandma that way....we're going to go." I ushered her out of the room screaming (my daughter was the one screaming, although I wanted to). As I carried her to a private space where she could melt down with me safely, it hit me — we'd been traveling for six or seven hours. Of course she's exhausted and just letting me know in her four-year-old way. Duh. My fault again.

I cannot count the number of times my children's behavior has hit the skids because they were suddenly overtaken by hunger just twenty minutes after they'd been offered food. And their inevitable response — "I wasn't hungry then" — always seemed so unfair. Apparently all is fair when it comes to love, war, and toddlers.

2. Clarity, please. Children will often push our limits simply because they haven't received a straight answer to the question, "What will you do if I do such-and-such?" And then they might need to know, "Will it be different on Monday afternoon? What about when you're tired? Or I'm cranky? If I get upset, will you do something different?"

So by continuing to push limits, toddlers are only doing their job, which is to learn about our leadership (and our love), clarify our expectations and house rules, and to understand where their power lies. Our job is to answer as calmly and directly as possible. Our responses will obviously vary from situation to situation, but they should consistently demonstrate that we're totally unthreatened by their behavior, that we can handle it, and that it's no big deal at all.

3. What's all the fuss about? When parents lose their cool, lecture, over-direct, or even *talk* about limit-pushing behaviors a bit too much, they can create interesting little dramas which children are compelled to re-enact. Punishments and emotional responses create stories that are frightening, alarming, shaming, guilt-inducing, or any combination.

When parents say more than a sentence or two about the limit-pushing behavior, even while remaining calm, they risk creating a tale about a child with a problem (perhaps he hugs his baby sister too forcefully), which then causes the child to identify with this as *his* story and problem, when it was just an impulsive, momentary behavior he tried out a couple of times.

For instance, counter to the example I shared about my daughter speaking rudely to Grandma, which for me clearly indicated that she was out-of-herself and unraveling, my response would be far more minimal if a spark of rudeness was directed at me. Rather than react and risk creating a story around occasional whining, screaming "you're stupid," "I hate you," etc., I would *dis*-empower those behaviors by allowing them to roll-l-l off my back.

Perhaps I'd acknowledge, "I hear how angry you are about leaving the park. That really disappointed you."

Always, always, always encourage your child to express these feelings.

Again, testing us with these behaviors from time

to time is age-appropriate, and if we react, we may encourage this to continue.

Sometimes children will smile or laugh when they know they are re-enacting a story, but this is usually an uneasy, tentative smile rather than one of happiness.

4. Do I have capable leaders? Imagine how disconcerting it is to be two, three, or four years old and not be certain we have a stable leader. The most effective leaders lead with confidence, keep their sense of humor, and make it look easy. This takes practice but — not to worry — children will give us plenty of chances through their limit-pushing behavior until we get it right. As Magda advises:

"Know what's important, both for you and for the child. If you are not clear, the child's opposition will persist, which will make you, the parent, even angrier. This in turn highlights the conflict that exists already, leading to an unhappy situation combining anger, guilt, and fear. A child has a difficult time growing up with ambivalent parents."
— Magda Gerber, *Dear Parent: Caring for Infants With Respect*

5. I've got a feeling. Children will sometimes persistently push limits when they have internalized feelings and stress that they need to release. Trusting this invaluable process and calmly (but firmly) holding the limits for our child while welcoming his or her feelings is the quickest and healthiest way to ease this need for limit-pushing (details and an example in Chapter 20). Maintaining an "all feelings allowed" attitude will nip most limit-pushing behaviors in the bud.

6. The sincerest form of flattery (sort of). Children are sensitive and impressionable, and we are their most influential models, so they will absorb our behavior and reflect it through theirs. For example, if we snatch toys away from our child, she may persistently snatch from friends. A child is likely to behave more erratically whenever her parents are upset or stressed about anything, especially if her parents haven't openly shared these feelings.

7. Seems the best way to get your attention these days. If the comfort and validation of our attention has been in short supply, or if there have been compelling mini-stories and dramas created around our child's limit-pushing behavior, she might end up repeating them to seek this negative attention.

8. Have you told me that you love me lately? When children feel ignored, or even just a bit out of favor with us, it rattles them, and fear shows up in their limit-pushing behavior. Reassuring hugs, kisses, and "I love you" will certainly help to mend these bridges, but the messages of love that matter most are heard through our patience, empathy, acceptance, respectful leadership, and the genuine interest we take in knowing our child.

To love toddlers is to know them.

3.

Talking to Toddlers

Toddlers are often talked about as if they are a species unto themselves. And when we're in the thick of it — the testing, mood swings, and meltdowns (ours and theirs) — we may indeed feel in alien territory.

Fear not! Toddlers are just small humans in turmoil, easily thrown off-balance due to rapid growth, thrilled by new abilities and accomplishments, but often frustrated by all they still can't do or say.

Here are some simple communication adjustments we can make to help ease frustration and foster trust:

1. Talk normally. Children want to learn *our* language. Avoid baby talk and speak in full sentences so that you are modeling the language you want your child to adopt right from the beginning. This feels more respectful and natural to us, too. We can maximize comprehension by making our sentences shorter, slowing down our speech, and pausing after each sentence to give our infant or toddler the time he needs to absorb our words.

Ignore the advice of a popular expert who tells you to imitate your toddler with Neanderthal 'ape talk' — as if talking *down* to a toddler like he is mentally deficient is the only way he can understand us.

Imagine going to a foreign country, courageously attempting to speak the language, and then being mocked with an imitation of your awkward wording. Would you get in a foreigner's face and ape his pidgin English? Toddlers have been immersed in our language for many, many months and comprehend volumes more than they can speak.

2. Turn *no* into *yes*. In a recent parent/toddler class, Kendra asked me what she should do when her vibrant 19 month-old daughter interrupted discussions with her husband. She said that telling Audrey not to interrupt wasn't working at all. I suggested she say, "Audrey, I hear you asking for our attention. When Daddy and I are finished talking I am going to listen only to you. Please give us five minutes." (And then follow through.)

Will this response work miracles in every situation? Probably not. Children never seem to outgrow the need for our attention when we're busy. But making a toddler feel heard, rather than telling her "no" and "don't" all the time, respects her need to save face and makes her more likely to respond with compliance.

Similarly, telling a child, "I want you to sit still on my lap," instead of "Don't bounce on me!" seems to lessen a toddler's urge to test. Children appreciate positive instruction and tend to tune out or resist the words "no" and "don't". Better to save those words for emergencies.

3. Real choices. Offering a toddler an option like, "Are you going to put the toy away on the shelf or in the box?" is another variation of turning a toddler's perceived negative (the child must put the toy away) into a positive (she gets to choose where to place it). Or we might say, "I see you're still playing. Would you like to change your diaper now, or in five minutes?"

Deciding between two options is usually all a toddler needs, as long as the question is an easy one. "What should we have for dinner?" or "What are you going to wear today?" are big questions and can be overwhelming. Be careful of giving false choices like: "Do you want to go to Aunt Mary's house?" We're left with egg on our faces when our toddler answers, "No!"

4. First, acknowledge. Acknowledging an infant or toddler's point-of-view can be magically calming, because it provides something he desperately needs – the feeling of being understood. A simple affirmation of our child's struggles, "You are having a hard time getting those shoes on. You're really working hard," can give him the encouragement he needs to persevere through his frustration.

Be careful not to assume a child's feelings: "You're afraid of the dog"; or to invalidate the child's response because we view it as overreaction: "It's just a doggy. He won't hurt you." It is safest to state only what we know for certain. "You seem upset by the dog. Do you want me to pick you up?"

Acknowledging first can take the bite out of not getting one's way. "You want to play longer outside, but now it's time to come in. I know it's hard to come in when you're not ready." And no matter how wrong or ridiculous our child's point-of-view might seem to us, he needs the validation of our understanding.

Acknowledging our child's desires means expressing truths we might rather ignore like, "You wanted to run across the street. I won't let you." Or, "You want to leave Aunt Lucy's house, but it isn't time yet. "

It's always hardest to remember to acknowledge a child in the heat of a difficult moment, but if a child can hear anything during a temper tantrum, it reassures him to hear our recognition of his point-of-view. "You wanted an ice cream cone and I said 'no'. It's upsetting not to get what you want."

When a toddler feels understood, he senses the empathy behind our limits and corrections. He still resists, cries, and complains, but at the end of the day, he knows we are with him, always in his corner. These first years will define our relationship for many years to come.

4.

Baby Discipline: Person to Person

Hi Janet:

My question is about my almost-13-month-old son. He is extremely curious and engaged in the world around him. We have always tried to empower him and make him feel safe and supported to try anything and everything (within safety, of course).

Drawing from my experiences working as an educator in a school that was very much inspired by Reggio Emilia and Montessori, I try to speak to him in terms of what he can do instead of what he can't do, and this involves very little – if any – use of the word "no." I also try to speak in a neutral, even-keeled tone, acknowledge his emotions by making observations rather than quick assumptions (i.e. "You seem frustrated. May I help you? etc."), and utilize the power of gentle touch.

Lately, I've been hearing from friends about discipline and how at this age, our little ones are testing us and we shouldn't be reinforcing any "bad habits" such as yelling/loud verbalizations, whining for things, and doing things we don't want them to do. I understand that our responses to our children send powerful messages. Personally, I find that compared to my friends, I give my son very few limits and restrictions. As long as something seems physically and socially/emotionally safe, I allow him to try and examine whatever grabs his interest. I feel proud that he is curious and eager to engage and explore.)

What are your thoughts on disciplining an early toddler?

Thank you!

Dena

Dena's note is an articulate description of a critical moment in both her child's emotional development and the foundation of a healthy, respectful parent/toddler relationship. This was my response:

Dear Dena:

It sounds like your instincts, experience, and education have helped you develop an extremely positive relationship with your son. You have obvious adoration for him and are rightfully proud, and you also view him as a capable individual and treat him that way. This is evident by the way you:

a) stay calm and neutral when he is frustrated;

b) tell him what he is *allowed* to do, rather than wearing out the word "no";

c) acknowledge his feelings and point-of-view even when they are in disagreement with you or with a rule; and

d) keep him safe while being careful not to discourage his curiosity.

You're right on track for establishing a relationship of trust and respect that will make discipline an organic, intuitive, less baffling part of parenting your toddler.

I agree with your friends about young toddlers needing behavioral boundaries, but the way we establish those limits and respond to our child's healthy impulse to test them is what makes all the difference. As you say, our responses send powerful messages. Every interaction we have with our child is a learning experience, and that's why I recommend the respectful "person to person" approach you are taking.

Here are my thoughts and suggestions about early toddler discipline. Since you brought up "yelling/loud verbalizations and whining," I'll try to use those behaviors as a running example.

Our needs matter, too. Parenting is about developing a relationship with another person. We make many worthwhile sacrifices when we are raising children, but it's best to not subjugate all our needs to keep our child happy, because a) doing so makes *us* feel unhappy and resentful; and b) it doesn't give our children a healthy attitude towards discipline or a realistic expectation about life.

Beginning an honest, respectful approach to discipline means owning our space in a relationship with our babies. Just as we are learning about our children, they need to know *us* — our likes and dislikes, our pet peeves, our limits. We need to get comfortable disagreeing with each other, and infants and toddlers express disagreement by crying or having a tantrum.

These are *not* the urgent cries of pain, distress, or hunger that we would drop everything to address, but they are no less difficult to hear. To develop an honest, balanced person-to-person relationship, our children need to learn early on that we will do our best to give them everything they need, but that they can't always get what they want... and that's okay.

For some of us, that might mean demanding a few

personal minutes in the morning to have a cup of coffee, take a quick glance at the newspaper, go to the bathroom on our own, or spend a little time in the kitchen preparing their food or ours. Then, holding up our end of the bargain means allowing our child to express his feelings while we stay calm and acknowledge:

"You're upset about how long I'm taking in the kitchen."

"You don't want me to go."

"I hear you calling me. I'll be there in five more minutes."

"I know you want to climb on me to practice standing, but that's bothering me. I'm going to help you sit down again."

In the case of a 13-month-old whining or yelling, you could say, "That's too loud. I can't understand you when you yell (whine, etc.). Are you asking me to pick you up? I can't do that right now, but I'll sit with you for a few minutes when I'm done putting the groceries away."

With an older, more verbal child, you might say, "Please speak in your regular voice so that I can understand." Or, "That yelling is hurting my ears. Please stop and talk to me. Tell me what you want."

So, we are not ignoring the whining or yelling, but we're not accommodating it either. We're guiding our child to tell us what he needs as clearly and politely as he can, and then letting him know what we are willing and able to do in response.

Clear expectations. From the beginning our job is to make our expectations as clear and consistent as possible. The best way to do this is to give babies predictable, routine kinds of days. A daily rhythm helps them to eat, sleep, and play better, and to feel a little control over their world. Rested and fed, babies are much more amenable to our guidance, less likely to feel overwhelmed and misbehave. (Often whining or yelling = tired, hungry or over-stimulated.)

Direct, honest, first person communication. A good way to remember to treat our baby like a person is to talk to him in the first person. Using "I" and "you" instead of "Mommy" and "Joey" works wonders to keep our communication direct and honest. And it's much easier for our toddler to understand and respond to our guidance when we say calmly, "I don't want you to hit me" rather than "Mommy doesn't want Joey hitting her," or "We don't hit," or "We don't yell" (while the child might be thinking, "Well, I do!").

Don't "just say no". Our babies sense our respect and learn far more about us and our expectations when we use "no" sparingly and replace it with simple guidance and a brief explanation: "Please don't hit the dog. That hurts her. You can hit this stuffed animal"; "I can't let you touch the electric cord. It's not safe. I'm going to help you let go of it"; or "I don't want you to yell. It hurts my ears, and I can't understand you. Please show me what you want." Children are also more inclined to listen to "no" when we don't say it all the time.

Guidance not gimmicks. Giving person-to-person guidance means saying "no" to gimmicks, tactics, and punishments like time-out. It means not giving distractions or the silent treatment to a child who is yelling, whining (or otherwise misbehaving) to discourage the behavior, but rather asking her directly what she wants to communicate and telling her how we'd like her to say it.

I don't recommend toddler lingo like "inside voice" and "use your words." Why? *Because we would never say those things to another adult.* (And asking ourselves, "Would I treat an adult this way?" is a good gauge for ensuring respect for our child.) Neither would we bribe or distract peers to control their behavior.

Dealing with our toddler as a person means insisting he hold our hand when we are walking together rather than leashing or chasing him, and expecting him to sit when he eats and not throw his food. Toddlers are definitely capable of cooperating, but they need to be taught through respectful feedback, corrections, and modeling rather than being tricked, manipulated, or coerced.

Curiosity rocks. Don't discourage it. Our instinct as parents is to say, "Oh no, don't do that" when our toddler surprises us by suddenly being able to reach or climb onto something 'out of bounds'. But our children's abilities are developing daily, and we don't want to discourage them. Remembering to say, "Wow, you can reach that now!" or "Look at the leaf you found," before adding "but this isn't safe for you to touch (or put in your mouth). I'm going to move it," encourages our baby to continue following his healthy instinct to explore.

Continuing the example of annoying vocalizations, that might mean saying to infants (who go through charming phases in which they experiment vocally), "You can make that loud crowing sound now! Wow, that's ear-splitting!" And then you'll probably just leave it at that, because if you say too much, or try to discourage a young infant's enthusiastic noise-making, you might fuel the fire. Sometimes, we need the self-discipline to know when to hold our breath and bite our tongue.

I hope this helps.

Warmly,

Janet

5.

A Toddler's Need for Boundaries

When an infant approaches the end of his first year, parents begin to struggle with boundaries. Soft-hearted parents allow a child to climb all over them in my parent/infant class. The child is searching for limits and boundaries for his behavior. But moms and dads are often afraid to say, "I don't want you to climb on me. You can sit with me. If you need to climb, there is a climbing structure over there."

The sooner a caregiver can establish those limits, the easier it will be for the child to relinquish "testing" and return to playing. Parents sometimes fear they will crush a child's spirit if they are firm and consistent about rules. Truthfully, it is the other way around. A child does not feel free unless boundaries are clearly established.

Educator Janet Gonzalez-Mena used the following analogy to describe a child's need for boundaries: Imagine driving over a bridge in the dark. If the bridge has no railings, we will drive across it slowly and tentatively. But if we see railings on either side of us, we can drive over the bridge with ease and confidence. This is how a young child feels in regard to limits in his environment.

Seeking the "railings" he needs to feel secure, a child will continue to test a caregiver until boundaries are clearly stated. Power struggles are a necessary part of the development of self for the child; however, the outcome must be that the child knows that the adult is in charge. Children do not usually admit this, but they do not wish to be all powerful, and the possibility that they might be is frightening indeed. Children raised without firm, consistent boundaries are insecure and world-weary. Burdened with too many decisions and too much power, they miss out on the joyful freedom every child deserves.

In the parenting classes at RIE, it is not uncommon for a toddler to act out by hitting, pushing, or throwing an object at a parent or at another child. When this problem arises, I encourage the parent, if he or she is able to anticipate the hit, to raise a hand to block the child's aggression and say firmly but matter-of-factly, "I won't let you hit." Or, right after the strike, a parent might simply say, "I don't want you to hit."

If parents show anger, become agitated, or say too much, they risk turning the child's undesirable behavior into an event. For instance, if a parent begins to lecture, "It's not nice to hit! Hitting hurts people! We don't hit in our family," the parent may fuel the fire by giving too much attention to the child's action and unwittingly cause the child to want to repeat it.

In the other extreme, if a parent responds with "Oh no! Please don't hit me, okay?" or "We don't hit our friends, do we?" the child is not receiving the clear authority that he requires. The child will then keep testing to prompt the parent to take charge.

When children act out, I imagine them holding up little red flags that say: "Help!"; "Stop me!"; "Rein me in!"; or "Parent me!"

A parent needs to respond with clarity,

composure, and conviction.

If a child who is signaling a need for boundaries is not dealt with consistently and effectively, the child may resort to waving bigger red flags. I witnessed a big flag years ago when my three-year-old daughter and I were walking near a park playground. A boy who looked four or five ran around the entire perimeter of the playground to approach her and hit her on the chest. She did not cry, but we were both stunned.

In other circumstances, I might have been thrilled at what then came into view. A handsome and famous James Bond type movie star rushed towards me. He was the boy's mortified father, who, unable to look me in the eye, mumbled a cursory apology and ushered his son away.

While all parents have to learn and adapt to understand how to best guide a child's behavior, the absence of such guidance can have serious, long-term consequences. If these issues are left untended, a child might eventually experiment with destructive behavior, inflicting damage on others or himself as an unconscious call for parental intervention. It is always safest to deal with limits effectively at the earliest possible stage.

What we have in the beginning, though, is our adorably angelic baby. We are shocked when she first shows any sign of aggression. Most toddlers act out at some point, and a parent need not worry that the child is demonstrating an evil streak! In fact, children often misbehave to signal that they are tired and need to go home.

A toddler also acts out when there is a blatant failure to draw clear boundaries at home. Sometimes, the child is exposed to adults or older children who do not respect the toddler's boundaries; they grab and tickle him, for example, depriving him of a sense of secure space. When a young child is overpowered and assaulted in this way, he becomes confused about physical boundaries with other people. If parents or older children feel a need to roughhouse with the baby, they should wait until he is old enough to be a more equal partner.

Sometimes a child will suddenly act out in class because there are gaps in his 'railings' at home. Henry's story aptly demonstrates the intensity of a child's need for thorough boundaries as he grows in independence:

Henry is a charming, gregarious twenty-month-old who greets parents as they come to class and hands toys to children who seem distressed. But one day Henry came to class and started to hit everyone. Henry's mother, Wendy, was beside herself with worry. I asked Wendy if anything was different at home, and she mentioned that she was frustrated while getting Henry to sit in his car seat when it was time to go somewhere. She was allowing Henry to do it in his own time, waiting while he played around inside the car. Wendy said she finally became impatient, and after telling him what she would do, she placed him in his seat. She could not believe that Henry cried anyway, even after she had tried to be respectful, giving him so much time to sit in the seat himself!

Wendy was confusing a transitional situation, a time when Henry needed to feel his mother was in control, with play time, a time when a child is best left to direct what will happen. I advised Wendy to give Henry the option of climbing into his seat by himself, but if he did not climb in right away, she should place him in his seat, even if he cried. Wendy sent me a thankful note a few days later. When Wendy made it clear to Henry that it was not up to him to decide when to sit in his car seat, his need to red-flag his mother was abated. Henry had stopped hitting.

The clearest proof that I have ever found of a child's desire for parental control came through a friend of mine and also involved a car seat. Holly was a tentative mom, someone who avoided setting limits. Holly told me she was having an impossible time getting three-year-old Eliza to sit in her car seat. Eliza screamed and refused to cooperate. I recommended to Holly that she say, "I know you don't want to, but you must sit in your car seat" and then place Eliza into the car seat as gently and calmly as she could. Holly reported back to me that when she had insistently placed Eliza in the car seat, Eliza kicked and screamed. Then, as Holly started the car in complete dismay, Eliza said softly, "That's what I wanted you to do."

Children do not feel hurt when the adults they desperately need establish behavioral boundaries. It is easier for a parent to indulge a child than it is to be firm and consistent, and children know that. A child may cry, complain or even throw a tantrum when limits are set. In their hearts, however, children sense when a parent is working ardently to provide a safe nest and real love.

6.

The Key to Cooperation

A sing-a-long to the tune of "My Favorite Things" from *Mary Poppins*:

Wiping wet noses and nails that need clipping - Changing soiled diapers and medicine sipping - Sitting in car seats, injections that sting - These are a few of my favorite things...

... Said no child, *ever*. And since children are inclined to resist these activities, parents tend to dread them. So in our haste to get the job done, we rush our babies through diaper changes and lunge at their snotty noses. We distract kids in order to slip them their medicine and keep them still when they need shots. We attempt to cut their nails and hair when they aren't looking, maybe even while they sleep.

Ironically, these tactics end up *creating* unpleasantness and increasing the resistance we'd hoped to avoid. Our babies learn quickly to run for the hills every time we approach them with a tissue.

But there's a simple secret that eases the pain of these mundane duties and can even transform them into enjoyable times of cooperation and connection.

The secret to enlisting our children's cooperation is

the same for all aspects of successful parenting: **respect.**

Newborns, infants, toddlers, and preschoolers — people of all ages — want to be engaged with, included, and invited to participate rather than have things done *to* them. Who can blame us? Here are some key ways to offer respect:

1. Make the activity a familiar routine and/or give advance notice. Life can seem overwhelming to young children. The more they know going in, the more likely they'll view an activity positively and be able to rise to the occasion.

We inform children two ways: a) by developing predictable daily routines so they know what to expect; and b) by talking honestly about everything that will happen (at the doctor's office, for example) ahead of time.

"Predictability is habit forming. Developing habits makes it much easier to live with rules. Because very young children do not understand the reasons behind the rules they are expected to follow, it is better if these rules become simply a matter of course. There are some things we do not need or want to re-examine every time we do them, such as brushing our teeth."
    – Magda Gerber, *Dear Parent: Caring for Infants With Respect*

2. Don't interrupt. Respect your child's play and other chosen activities. Don't interrupt unless absolutely necessary. Oftentimes, we realize that the runny nose or wet diaper can wait until the child is finished, or at least has a bit more time. Again, prepare children: "In a few minutes it will be time to change into your PJ's, brush teeth and chose a book."

"If a child has ample opportunity to play independently, without interruption, he is likely to be much more willing to cooperate with the demands of his parent."

– Magda Gerber

3. Communicate with even the youngest infants. Children are whole people from birth, and we encourage their participation and partnership in tasks when we speak to them honestly and directly: "I need to wipe your nose with this tissue. Please keep your head still for a moment."

4. Offer autonomy. Let your child do it — or at least try. What's there to lose? You might be amazed by your baby's nose wiping talents. Children of toddler age and older feel more autonomous when we offer them choices: "Would you like to take your medicine now or after lunch?" "Which fingernail shall we clip first?"

But beware of false choices. It might seem more polite and respectful to ask children, "Can I give you your medicine now?", but only if all options are acceptable to us.

5. Slow everything down. Slow down movements, words, and the time in between them. The younger the child, the more time they need to process our words.

"One can further enhance the child's sense of himself as a decision-maker by allowing enough time to elapse after requesting something, so that the child can decide on his

own whether or not to cooperate."

– Magda Gerber

6. Don't multitask. Children need our undivided attention during these cooperative activities. Pay attention, connect, and encourage children to do the same.

7. Acknowledge. If we are approaching the situation respectfully and our children still resist or object, acknowledge their feelings and point-of-view: "You are turning your head away. You don't want me to dry your nose with the tissue. I'll wait a little for you to be ready."

When, despite our respectful attitude, children refuse to cooperate and we must force the (t)issue, it's even more crucial that we acknowledge their disagreement or anger: "You didn't like that. It upset you."

8. Give thanks. Thank children for helping rather than offering empty "good job" praise. Acknowledge accomplishments and progress: "Now you are able to brush your own teeth!"

Chelsea wrote a note to me sharing how she ended a "spoon fight" with her 10-month-old baby by communicating with him respectfully, slowing down, and offering him autonomy:

... Every time I tried to give our baby puréed food he would reach for the spoon and hold on to it so tight that his knuckles would turn white. I would get so annoyed and would try to peel it from his hands. Feedings were getting

more and more stressful. I thought the only solution would be offering more finger foods, but there were times when I needed to give him puréed food.

About a month ago I had my 'a-ha' moment and realized I was approaching this all wrong. I asked for the spoon. He didn't give it to me, but he did eventually drop it. I asked if it was for me. He stared. I reached for it and explained I would put more food on the spoon and give it back.

Over the next few meals we started to master giving the spoon to each other. Now he gives the spoon — no big deal. And not only the spoon — now he likes to give me everything, rocks, toys, whatever!

Mealtime has changed 100%, and I feel like my boy actually enjoys giving to others when he wants to. Thank you for all the time you put into your writing. It has helped me as a parent so much.

7.

5 Reasons to Ditch the Distractions (And What To Do Instead)

Distraction is a popular "redirection" tactic for dealing with an infant or toddler's undesirable behavior. Its appeal is understandable, because it's about aiming a child to another activity rather than confronting an issue directly. It helps us dodge the bullet of our child's resistance, which might include anger, tears, or a total meltdown (and we're all eager to avoid those things, especially in public).

Apparently, distraction often works — at least momentarily — and I can appreciate that it allows mom, dad, or caregiver to remain the good guy. I love being the good guy! Instead of saying, "I can't let you draw on the sofa. Here's some paper if you want to draw," (or better yet, not leaving young children unsupervised with markers in the first place), it's easier and less likely to cause friction if I change the subject enthusiastically: "Can you draw me a silly face on this piece of paper?"

So, I may save my sofa in the nick of time, but my child has no idea that drawing on it is *not* okay, and he may very well try it again. Well, at least there are no tears, and I'm still the good guy!

And right there is the first of several problems I

have with distraction:

1. Phoniness. I don't like acting perky and upbeat when I'm really a little annoyed. Besides making me feel like a big phony, I don't think it's good modeling or healthy for my relationship with my children. As uncomfortable as it is to face the music (or markers on the sofa), I believe children deserve and *need* an honest response. No, we shouldn't react angrily if we can possibly help it, but we don't have to perform or be inauthentic either. Staying calm and giving a simple correction and a real choice (like "You can draw on paper or find something else to do.") is all that's needed.

Yes, the child may get upset — he has a right to his conflicting opinion and his feelings. It's good for him to vent and for us to acknowledge, "You really wanted to draw on the sofa and I wouldn't let you." Children are capable of experiencing these kinds of safe, age-appropriate conflicts. Which brings me to my second objection to distraction...

2. Wastes opportunities to learn from conflict. Our children need practice handling safe disagreements with us and with peers. When our infant or toddler is struggling with a peer over a toy and we immediately suggest, "Oh, look at this cool toy over here...," we rob him of a valuable opportunity to learn how to manage conflicts himself.

Directing our child to another identical toy, if there is one, might be helpful if children seem really stuck, but even then the infant or young toddler usually wants the one that has 'heat' in another child's hands. Often the children are far more interested in understanding the struggle than they are in the particular toy. But whatever their focus, young children need time and our confidence in them to learn to resolve conflicts rather than avoiding them.

3. No guidance. What does a child learn when we direct him to draw a silly face rather than just telling him we can't let him draw on the sofa? Infants and toddlers need us to help them understand the house rules and eventually internalize our expectations and values. Distraction erases the possibility of a teachable moment.

4. Underestimates and discourages attention and awareness. Distracting a child means asking him to switch gears and forget what has taken place. Is this lack of awareness something to encourage? An article I read recently (published by a university press) suggests: "Since young children's attention spans are so short, distraction is often effective."

Even if I agreed about children having short attention spans, which I don't, distracting them from what they are engaged in seems a sure fire way to make them even shorter. And children who aren't used to distraction don't buy it. They can't be fooled, coaxed, or lured away from marking up the sofa (unfortunately). Encouraged to be fully present and aware, they need a straight answer or directive, and they deserve one.

An aware child may be less convenient sometimes (when we can't trick him with sleight of hand, "Oops, the cell phone disappeared, here's a fun rattle instead!"), but awareness and attentiveness are essential to learning and will serve him well throughout his life.

5. Respect. Distracting is trickery that underestimates a toddler's intelligence — his ability to learn and comprehend. Toddlers deserve the same respect we would give an adult rather than this (from a website about parenting toddlers):

Distract and divert. The best form of toddler discipline is redirection. First, you have to distract them from their original intention and then, quickly divert them toward a safer alternative. Give them something else to do for example, helping with the household chores and soon they will be enjoying themselves rather than investing a lot of emotional energy into the original plan.

How distraction can be construed as discipline is beyond me. More importantly – would you distract an adult in the middle of a disagreement and direct her to mop up the floor? Then why treat a younger person like a fool? I believe that we can trust babies to choose where to invest their emotional energy. Only babies know what they are working on and figuring out.

Here are some alternative responses that not only work, but also feel respectful and authentic:

Breathe first. Pause and observe... unless there is a marker making contact with our sofa or a fist making contact with our toddler's buddy's head, in which case we quickly take hold of the hands and/or markers as gently as possible. But then we breathe.

Remain calm, kind, empathetic, but firm. In the

case of a peer conflict, narrate the situation objectively without assigning blame or guilt. Magda Gerber called this *sportscasting*: "Jake and John are both trying to hold onto the truck. It's tough when you both want to use the same thing... You're really having a hard time..." Allow the struggle, but don't let the children hurt each other. "I see you're frustrated, but I won't let you hit."

Acknowledge feelings and point-of-view. When it's over, acknowledge, "Jake has the truck now. John, you wanted it. You're upset." Be fully available to respond with comfort if the child wants it.

After our response to a behavior like drawing on the sofa, and after we've allowed the child to cry, argue, or move on as he chooses, while offering empathy and comfort, we can acknowledge his point-of-view: "You thought the sofa needed decorating. I said no, and you didn't like that."

Recognize achievement and encourage curiosity. The use of distraction as redirection reflects our natural tendency to want to put an immediate end to a child's undesirable behavior. And in our haste, it's easy to forget to recognize and encourage positives in the situation – positives like inventiveness, achievement, curiosity. When the situation *isn't* an emergency, we can take a moment to acknowledge: "Wow, you reached all the way up to the counter and picked up my sunglasses!"

Then we can allow the child to examine the sunglasses while we hold them. If he tries to take them out of our hands, we might say, "You can look at these and touch them, but I won't let you take them." Then, if that turns into a struggle, we might say finally, "You really want to hold these yourself and I can't let you. I'm going to put them away in the desk."

Dealing with these situations openly with patience, empathy, and honesty — braving a child's tears and accepting temporary 'bad guy' status — is the path to a loving relationship, trust, and respect. This, believe it or not, is *real* quality time.

8.

Why Children Won't Follow Our Directions

Parents often ask me, "Why won't my kids listen?" What they *really* mean is, "Why won't they follow my directions?"

Children are ready to listen, primed from birth to begin decoding our words and intuiting our unspoken messages. They are also unique individuals who quickly develop ideas, opinions, and wills of their own. Babies and toddlers often understand exactly what we want but choose to do the opposite.

So why won't our kids just do as we ask? Here are the most common reasons:

1. Disconnection. Children feel disconnected for a variety of reasons. Perhaps we've been punitive or manipulative (sometimes without even knowing it), rather than the respectful, benevolent guides our children need in order to learn our expectations.

We might have made the common mistake of taking our child's age-appropriate resistant behavior personally. How could this child for whom we do everything, and have essentially given our lives, deliberately disobey or disappoint us (hit her baby brother, for example) when we've told her hundreds of times. Does she not love us?

Children often repeat their resistant and rebellious behaviors because they aren't feeling our love. They sense they are out of favor with us — misunderstood and blamed when what they need is our help. Our behavior control tactics (usually applied with a dose of anger or frustration) can make our children uncomfortable, confused, and even fearful, and this is manifested in their increasingly erratic behavior.

These impulsive behaviors tend to continue and repeat themselves until we recognize the intense message our kids are sending us: *Be my gentle leader and help me feel safe again.*

2. Words are not enough. Parents are often taken aback when their adorable 11-month-old infant hits them in the face and then smiles and does it again after they say, "Ow! No, we don't hit, " or "You're hurting me!" Has this baby suddenly become evil or stopped loving us? Of course not. She is simply expressing something she cannot verbalize, and this is a crucial time to demonstrate that we have a handle on these behaviors, that we've got her back.

We show her by calmly holding her flailing hands while assuring, "I won't let you hit me. That hurts." And if our little one is in our arms and continues to flap at us, we might add, "You're having a hard time not hitting, so I will put you down."

Then, perhaps, after placing our child down she bursts into tears. Since we've taken the action necessary to prevent her from upsetting us, we now have the presence of mind to realize, *Ah-ha, Josie didn't sleep well last night, and even though it's too early for her usual naptime, she's exhausted. That's her message, and no wonder she wouldn't stop hitting.*

Once we've understood that our words are not enough for most young children (and how difficult it is for them to understand and express their needs), we see the ridiculousness of taking their refusals to follow our verbal directions personally. It's on us to make our expectations clear by following through with firm, but gentle actions.

3. Our reticence creates guilt. Sometimes, when parents believe their words should be enough, or when they are otherwise reticent to follow through, they try appealing to their child to do (or stop doing) whatever it is out of pity for them. For example, parents tell their child she "hurts their feelings" when she won't clean up the playroom, or they get vulnerable and cry whenever there are power struggles (which usually only happen when parents are reticent to take charge by setting a clear boundary).

These responses are not only ineffective, they can also make children feel guilty and cause an unhealthy sense of responsibility for (and, therefore, discomfort with) the vulnerable feelings of others.

4. We are unconvincing or way too exciting.

"If a parent does not really believe in the validity of a particular rule, or is afraid that the child will not obey, chances are the child will not."

– Magda Gerber

The manner in which we give directions will determine whether or not our children follow them.

Some parents need help perfecting their confident, matter-of-fact delivery, remembering to put a period (rather than a question like "okay?") at the end of their sentences.

Parents might also need to perfect what I call the "ho-hum stride" and use it to replace lunging towards the baby about to touch the dog's dish and shouting, "No!", or charging after the toddler who runs away when it's time to go home from the park (emergencies like running into traffic are a different story, of course). The moment we might save by rushing rather than sauntering confidently can cause numerous repetitions of the undesirable behavior, which has now become a thrilling game.

"Ho-hum responses" are also helpful when children whine, scream, or try out the profane new word they heard at preschool. Kids are much more likely to forget that word and stop whining or screaming if we *dis*-empower the behavior by ignoring it (which doesn't mean intentionally ignoring our child) or giving a ho-hum, nonchalant direction like "That's a bit too loud" or "That's an ugly word. Please don't use it."

5. We over-direct. No one likes being ordered around, especially when they are toddlers (or teenagers). Whenever possible, give children, including babies, choices and autonomy. Children desire to be active participants in life beginning at birth. Include toddlers in decisions and ask them to help you problem-solve. (Lisa Sunbury offers thoughtful suggestions in her article, "Let's Talk" at *Regarding Baby*)

Balancing our instructions with plenty of free play

time with children calling all the shots means they will be more willing to listen when we direct them. It also helps when we remember to always acknowledge our child's point-of-view, for example: "We've been having such a blast outside, and I understand not wanting to go back in, but we must."

6. Our child has better things to do. Sometimes not following directions is a good thing, because it reflects our child's healthy, delightful instinct to learn the way young children learn best — through play, exploration, and following inner-direction:

My daughter is 2.5 years old and when we go to activities (structured playgroups, mom/toddler stuff), she does not follow direction (or very rarely will follow direction). Maybe she will to a degree, but generally speaking, she is the wild flower that is rolling around, running, and dancing circles in the big open room while all the other kids are sitting quietly by their moms' side.... should I be concerned about this, or leave her to her own exploration (it's winter here so the big open space to run is a real treat!), or keep on trying to get her to listen to the 'animator' who is trying to run a session?

- Lenore

Hmm... Listen to an "animator" or roll, run, and dance? That's a tough one.

9.

The Choices Our Kids Can't Make

Respect is vital to parenting, but the word can confuse us, especially when it comes to setting limits with toddlers.

Children need lots of opportunities to be autonomous and have their choices respected. At the same time, they also need to know they're not in charge, and we demonstrate that through our confident, decisive, gentle leadership. It can be tricky figuring out how to balance these seemingly opposing needs. How do we know when our children should choose and when they need *us* to?

If our toddlers could let us know when we are giving them too much freedom and causing them to feel uncomfortably powerful, they probably wouldn't... at least, not verbally. But these uneasy feelings are usually expressed through our toddlers' behavior as they become more resistant, whiny, distracted, or clingy; or they continue to test until we give them the help they need. Meaning, until we make a choice for them.

It may seem ironic (and unfair!) that giving our children freedom to choose can cause them to test our boundaries even more, but there we are. Two-year-olds aren't terrible — they're torn. As much as they appear to want to be in charge, the reality of that power is frightening and can severely undermine their sense of security.

Most of the choices toddlers can't comfortably make are about transitions. This makes sense. Toddlers are already in the middle of a massive transition. They are growing and changing at a dizzying pace. Even the most minor transitions mean giving up the temporary balance they've managed to attain and finding their footing in a new situation.

When we give toddlers more than one brief choice during times of transition, we invite them to dig their heels in. Here's an example:

Your two-year-old has been invited to a party and suddenly, mysteriously, puts on the brakes as you approach the host's door. "No want to!" he whines.

You're thrown, or perhaps you've begun to expect this kind of behavior. You say to yourself, *"Well, what's the hurry? After all, we're only here for my boy to have a good time. I don't want him to be upset."*

So you wait with your child while he wanders around the front yard. You wait, wait, and wait some more for your child to tell you he's ready. You certainly don't want to enter your friend's house carrying a screaming child. And this should be his choice, right?

But because you are human, you're losing patience and getting annoyed (which is usually a sign that you need to set a limit). You try coaxing him with delectable descriptions of balloons, games, and yummy cake, all of which you know he adores. Still, he refuses. What now?

Pop Quiz

Should you:

a) Keep waiting, coaxing and getting more peeved?

b) Go back home?

c) Let him know it's time to go in, carry him inside and face his possibly explosive negative reaction?

d) Give him the choice of going in now or in three minutes (or perhaps the choice of walking or being carried) and then follow through with 'c'?

As you might have guessed, I recommend 'd'. Once you're inside, I'd allow the child to choose to stay on your lap for as long as he wishes, or to participate in the party, and be prepared to possibly repeat 'd' when it's time to leave (the joy!).

When we project calm, our children usually release their upset feelings quickly and feel free to move on. Which reminds me of a parenting rule of thumb: Fear (or even slight reticence) about upsetting, disappointing, or angering our children will cloud our vision and negatively affect our judgment.

The parents I know who have the most difficulty taking decisive action (even when they understand intellectually how much their children need it) are gentle, sensitive and sometimes over-identify with their children's feelings. (Ahem, do I seem to know this type well?)

Magda warned: *"A parent's ambivalence, guilt feelings, and areas of confusion in his or her role will be picked up and used amazingly fast by young children. They seem to have a sixth sense for it. Any ambivalence from a parent will produce a nagging response."*

Is this what we want for our children? Absolutely

not. Our kids are regularly going to resist our agendas, explode and meltdown on us. *That* is the freedom they need most. So, our job is to be a solid leader who can remain calm and empathetic in the face of our child's storms and not waver, get angry or pitying, or take his or her feelings personally.

"It's easier to say, 'Yes, okay, have your own way.' But then what has been accomplished?"

\- Magda Gerber

Here are some other instances when I believe children need us to gently and firmly overrule their choices and follow through:

1. Hurting themselves or others is an obvious one. Sometimes we can offer children the choice to hit or kick something safe, stomp their feet, or do something else to encourage them to safely get their feelings out. Always acknowledge the feelings, no matter how overly dramatic or inappropriate they might seem.

2. Repetitively taking toys is usually a sign that the child is asking for help with boundaries and needs to be gently stopped.

3. Car seats are a common source of struggle for parents. I don't believe that children feel comfortable choosing when (or if) they should get into the car seat. They *can* choose to get into the seat themselves or be helped.

4. Picking out clothing should be the child's prerogative within reason. But I don't believe in allowing children to go out in uncomfortable, revealing, or otherwise inappropriate clothing. For me, this is neglect, not respect.

5. Leaving our child to go wherever we need to go must be non-negotiable. Again, always acknowledge the child's feelings, assure her you'll be back, and then separate with calm conviction. It is torturous for a child to be in limbo attempting to keep us there longer while we waver.

If our children aren't getting the clear, consistent boundaries they need in one of these areas, their general sense of comfort and security can be diminished, which often causes them to test boundaries in other areas as well.

Navigating this delicate balance between freedom and boundaries is never easy (especially for those of us who aim to please), but these endless hard choices we make each day with our toddlers are a sure sign of our love. Deep down our children know that... and how much they need it.

10.

The Power of "No"

Hi Janet,

I am at a bit of a loss as to how to move forward with my son. He is 26 months and has recently started saying "no" to all of my requests, regardless of what they are.

My husband and I try very hard to pose our responses positively, avoiding "no" as much as possible. Rather than "no throwing food," we would say "please leave your food on your plate." So, we are not sure where this is coming from. I am hoping you have some advice.

One example is getting into his PJ's for bedtime. This is now taking well over half an hour because he just refuses to put them on. I am trying very hard not to force him and to give him as much opportunity to do it himself as possible, but it is making no difference. He is not throwing tantrums, just quite matter-of-factly saying "no" and then going about his business. I find myself just sitting there at a loss, not knowing what to do.

Thank you again for your wisdom.

Kate

Dear Kate:

This made me smile. "No" is *exactly* what your boy should be saying at this time of his life. It is a power word key to his burgeoning autonomy. He's feeling his independence. Don't let it rattle you in the least. In fact, welcome his differing opinion and acknowledge it. That's what he wants. Just don't give in to it.

So, when he says, "No, I don't want to put my PJ's on," stay calm. "Oh, I hear you. You don't want to put on your PJ's. What would you like to wear to bed?" Or maybe, "Which of these (2) PJ's will you wear?" Or "I hear you don't want to put on your PJ's. Perfectly understandable. But we won't have time for a book if you can't get them on in the next five minutes." Or "Would you like to put these on now, or in five minutes?"

The key is to continue to encourage his autonomy and give him options so that he doesn't feel bossed around. Be effortlessly in charge. Totally unthreatened. Worst case scenario: he sleeps with his regular clothes on.

Even then, you could always try, "I want you to be comfortable, so I'm going to help you put these pajamas on now. Or can you do it yourself?" Then you might say, "We don't have time for a book now because you didn't put your PJ's on in time, but hopefully tomorrow we'll get to bed a little earlier. I love you very much... Goodnight."

Saying, "Please leave the food on your plate," might work sometimes, but he may need options there, too. Throwing food is a pretty clear signal that he's not hungry. I don't believe that it's punitive to give children the boundary, "While you are eating, I want your food to stay on the plate. Throwing the food means you are done. I'm going to put the food away for later when you're hungry again."

Keep in mind that "no" is a very healthy, positive word for your boy to be experimenting with right now and a reflection of his secure attachment. You might even play a game with him where you offer him a bunch of choices (toys, clothes, food, whatever), and he gets to keep saying "no".

I remember spontaneously beginning a game like this with my toddler daughter when she was in the bath. She was playing with the bath toys, pouring water out of a cup or bottle. And when she hesitated a little before doing whatever it was, I said a big "no" in a way that she knew was teasing. Then she kept repeating the action and saying, "Say 'no' to me," with a big smile on her face. And I did, while acting *very* serious. She got to experience the powerful feeling of going against my wishes. That game became an instant favorite to be repeated at every bath. She couldn't get enough of it!

Hope this helps…

Cheers,

Janet

Hi Janet,

Thank you so much for the advice. I have been trying to give J choices, and it has made a world of difference. I gave him a choice of PJ's, a choice of two stories, that sort of thing. He has really responded well to having some options.

Also, it has been a big stress reliever for me. Yesterday morning he wouldn't get dressed. I gave him a choice of clothes, but he still refused. So I calmly said that I heard that he didn't want to get dressed right now and that I was going to make some breakfast, and when he was ready to get dressed to let me know and I would come and help him. He immediately said he was ready to get dressed and have breakfast. It takes a bit of practice, but we are both communicating better.

I try to be calm and respectful, but it is really helpful to

have the actual words to say. I did say exactly what you wrote. I felt prepared, J felt heard, and we are happier.
    Thanks again,
    Kate

11.

No Fan of Timers

"Kids seem to have all the time in the world — but adults don't. Even with an established routine, time is an abstract concept, especially to young children, so you can hardly expect them to share your sense of urgency. The solution: Get a timer. The bigger the numbers and the louder the ding, the better!"

– Nanny Stella, *Nickelodeon Parents Connect*

If you use a timer, I know what you're probably thinking, because I wrestled with it, too. *Why pick apart a tool that's working for us when you could be offering constructive advice? What could possibly be wrong with using timers? They help us set limits and deal with transitions more gracefully, and our kids love them.*

On the surface, timers are fun, effective, and innocuous, and I would certainly never criticize parents for using them. But my belief is that timers can also wind up (no pun intended) getting in our way, undermining a parent's ultimate goals.

So, I'm hoping you'll hear me out, which should take just a minute or two (go ahead and set your timer), and then feel free to disagree.

Finding our rhythm as competent leaders. Establishing ourselves as the confident, empathetic leaders our children need takes experience and plenty of practice. Setting limits and garnering cooperation are not anyone's favorite aspects of parenting, nor do they come naturally to most of us. So the appeal of a device that can play the bad guy and say it's time to stop playing outside on a warm summer evening is certainly understandable. But is it wise?

Personally, and as a parent coach, I've noticed that the more we practice confronting head-on our children's resistance to our limits, the more we get used to facing, accepting, and acknowledging their displeasure. Over time it gets easier, and we become more confident in our gentle leadership role. A timer in the mix to offset the "blame" is a crutch we don't need and can inhibit our progress in this area.

Gimmicks. Like my mentor Magda Gerber, I am not a fan of child care gimmicks of any kind, which is one reason (of many) that I avoid gadgets like walkers, jumpers, or bumbos; nor do I use bribes, tricks, sticker-charts, or even kiddy terminology like "time-out," "use your words," "big feelings," or "babywearing."

This may seem extreme, but I want everything I say and do in regard to my child to remind me 24/7 that he or she is nothing less than a whole person. I need the path of our person-to-person relationship to remain clear. It's hard enough to stay on track when there is such an astonishing lack of support in our society for respecting our youngest kids.

A reliable barometer for discerning whether a term or tactic is respectful is to ask ourselves if we would use it with an adult: Would we use a timer with anyone but a child or an egg? *(DING!) Time's-up for lounging around, Sweetheart, come help with the dishes!*

Your time has expired. *"Timers help give your kids a sense of time, and be more aware of the concept of time. This can only benefit them in the long run, not to mention help nip some of your daily battles in the bud now!"*

– Nanny Stella

Yes, a reasonable sense of time is important and good in the long run, but why the big rush to instill the concept at such an early age? I remember a concerned friend complaining that her child's Kindergarten used timers to move the children from learning center to learning center every five minutes which, unsurprisingly, unnerved her child rather than teaching him anything (except that school is impossibly stressful).

I'm sure that would be my reaction, as well, even as an adult. I imagine hearing that tick, tick, tick sound in anticipation of a loud ding, and I get anxious. (Might also explain why I'm rattled by jack-in-the-boxes.) And this distracting, panicky feeling would certainly kill the joy of any activity or train of thought I might be involved in. Perhaps timer-time is worse than no time at all?

One of the many mountains of things I treasure about young children is the total communion they have with time being relative. Kids lose themselves in time *all the time* and can inspire us to release ourselves from clocks, slow down, and join them. Why hurry children to learn the meaning of time when ignorance is such bliss?

"How did it get so late so soon?"

– Dr. Seuss

12.

Staying Unruffled

Toddlers are experts at ruffling our feathers, but these tiny people mean no disrespect. Testing our limits (and patience) is impulsive behavior on their part and a developmentally appropriate way to seek answers to important questions like:

Am I safe and cared for?
Do I have confident leaders?
Are they with me or against me?
Is it okay to want what I want, to feel what I'm feeling?
Am I a bad kid?

While probing those larger questions, toddlers are also asking us to clarify (and re-clarify) our expectations, to establish the house rules. For example:

What will my parents do if I... (hit the dog, push my sister, throw my food, put the brakes on when I'm supposed to be getting ready to leave the house)?
Is this decision mine or my parents'... (to go to bed, get into my car seat, hold my dad's hand in the parking lot)?

If we don't consistently give our toddlers the answers they need to feel guided, secure, and understood, they will usually need to continue asking through resistance and testing.

As parents we are not always able to ace these tests. We're human, we get tired and triggered, and that means we're going to lose our composure at least occasionally. That's okay. If we remain at least somewhat consistent, composed and clear, we'll get our messages across successfully.

Here are some suggestions that have helped me and the parents I've worked with over the years stay unruffled:

1. Gain perspective. Our attitude toward limit-pushing behavior is *everything*, and our perspective is what defines our attitude. Testing, limit-pushing, defiance and resistance are healthy signs that our toddlers are developing independence and autonomy. If we say "green," toddlers are almost *required* to say "blue," even if green is their favorite color, because if toddlers want what we want, they can't assert themselves as individuals.

Add to these challenges a lack of impulse control and general emotional turbulence, and you'll see why I recommend perceiving toddlers in this state more like mental health patients than unruly kids. Toddlers need our help, not anger or punishments.

And when they are experiencing stress, fear or other strong emotions, impulsive behaviors intensify. It's no surprise that the majority of the parents contacting me with behavior issues have a new baby, or are expecting one, or are dealing with some other major change that their child is reacting to.

Unfortunately, our toddlers aren't able to share their feelings about these situations on cue. Instead, they might share them by screaming "no!" in response to a direction, or melting down because we denied them one more cookie, or reacting melodramatically to some other seemingly insignificant disappointment. That's why we mustn't judge these overreactions, but rather try to understand and welcome them.

Instead of getting offended when our child screams because we've poured too much syrup on his pancakes, try to remember that this is really just an outlet for much deeper disappointments.

2. Perceive conflict and strong emotions positively (or, at least, a little less negatively). Many of us received the message as children that strong displays of emotion are unacceptable and conflicts are to be feared. Unfortunately, this perspective makes it next to impossible to stay unruffled with toddlers, who (as I explained above) *need* to disagree with us and feel safe expressing their strong emotions. Shifting this paradigm is one of our biggest challenges as parents, and yet enormously freeing.

We gradually make this shift when we practice acknowledging our child's point-of-view (for most of us the last thing we feel like doing when we are in conflict!). It needs to be perfectly okay for children to want what they want, even when we won't give it to them. No matter how unfair or ridiculous our child's stance seems, we don't coerce, argue, or judge.

3. Have reasonable expectations. Gaining perspective helps us to know what to expect. Then we aren't as inclined to set ourselves up to be surprised or offended when our child, for example, refuses to follow our most polite and reasonable directions, or won't stop trying to annoy us when we're making dinner, or demands more, more, more of whatever it is. What she actually needs is to explode.

During the toddler years, our most reasonable expectation is the unreasonable. Expecting the madness makes it far easier to keep our cool.

4. Be preventative, prepared, proactive. Our toddlers are naturally curious explorers, so placing them in situations in which this inclination is unwelcome is a set-up for mutual frustration. Also keep in mind that toddlers are easily over-stimulated and fatigued and can seem to go from full to famished in no time flat.

Being prepared and proactive means recognizing there's an excellent chance our toddlers are not going to follow our directions or agree to our limits. This doesn't mean we shouldn't proceed with confidence (we *need* to project confidence). It means we won't ask more than once, because that is a quick path to our annoyance and anger, and whenever the situation allows, we'll ask in a manner that gives our children a choice and a bit of time so that they can save face.

Remember that toddlers need to disagree to claim their new, more independent place in the world. In the toddler code book, compliance means weakness.

Then there's the back-up option: "Can you do this on your own, or will you need me to give you a helping hand?" This obviously isn't about what children can or can't do as much as what they are willing to do in that moment. If we are always ready for our toddlers to need a helping hand (no questions asked), we can remain unruffled, be firm and gentle rather than forceful and angry.

Don't anticipate willingness, and you won't be

disappointed.

And, by the way, toddlers aren't great at clearing up their toys and will usually need a helping hand, or a special basket, or a gentle logical consequence like "We can't take out more toys until we put these away."

5. Act as if... Integral to the parenting approach I teach is our authenticity as parents. But since handling our children's behavior issues non-punitively is a hugely important and noble goal that does not seem to come naturally to many of us, *acting as if* can definitely help.

Acting as if we're unruffled does not mean adopting stern expressions and voices or forcing laughter and games. It means imagining we've been handling these situations for so many years that we're completely calm and comfortable, so it's easy to be direct, definitive, and physically follow through when that's needed.

Once we begin to notice how effective we can be, we build the confidence we need to stop acting.

6. Use imagery. Three images that have worked for me are the CEO (Chapter 1), the superhero shield (Chapter 13), or even the teddy bear visual (Chapter 18). Use one of these or find a personal image that is confidence-building and helps you to feel calm and create the bit of emotional distance you need.

7. Practice — it gets easier. Each small success bolsters our confidence as parents, makes expressing our personal boundaries easier, and positively affects every relationship in our life.

8. Recognize personal triggers, projections, and weaknesses. Practicing self-reflection helps us to know our triggers (almost as well as our child does!), and then we can begin to understand them. Recognition is the first step toward change, and changing old patterns of response for the sake of our children is profoundly healing.

9. Find support. The toddler years are an intense time. To remain mostly unruffled, parents of toddlers need a shoulder to cry on, and some may need the support of a coach, counselor or therapist. Let your children be the inspiration to get the help you need.

13.

My Secret for Staying Calm When My Kids Aren't

I've hesitated to share this secret because I worry it seems silly. Then it occurred to me that if I'm really striving to provide a complete parenting toolbox, I can't *not* include a practice, however inane, that has been essential to my own sanity while raising three kids who are healthier and better adjusted than I could ever have hoped.

I'm the kind of person who absorbs and is affected by everyone's feelings, especially my kids'. But I also know that staying calm and centered in the face of even the darkest of my children's emotions is imperative to their well-being. My boat is easily rocked. I can lose perspective, and rather than giving my kids the solid support for their feelings or the behavior limits they need during a tantrum, I can end up losing patience, melting, second-guessing myself, getting mad or frustrated, yelling, and generally doing things that not only don't work, but also create problems that make matters worse.

When we lose our cool, most of what we say or do is completely lost on our children. All they learn when we're flailing is that they have the power to hurt us or ignite our rage, which unsettles them, creates an unsafe atmosphere, and usually causes them to repeat their difficult behaviors until and unless we find some control.

Or perhaps we say things like, "You're hurting my feelings!" Our vulnerability creates guilt and insecurity, burdening children with an inordinate amount of power and leaving them bereft of the confident, gentle leadership they desperately need.

But we're human. We're never going to like it when our kids are upset, and we're going to lose our cool sometimes. *More* than sometimes during the toddler years. How can we control our feelings and responses?

I appreciate the wonderful suggestions offered by parents, bloggers, and professionals for helping parents temper their emotional reactions — healthy things to do instead of yelling or spanking when we're triggered. A few of my favorites are: breathe; call a friend; do jumping jacks; and eat dark chocolate (preferably all at once). But in the frenzy of a difficult moment, I know *I* need something more immediate, powerful, and proactive.

So when my kids are angry, sad, frustrated, winding up or melting down, I imagine myself donning a superhero suit equipped with a protective shield that deflects even the fiercest, most irritating emotional outbursts. It makes me feel confident and capable and inspires me to rise above the fray. Just reaching for my superhero suit helps me to take a step out of myself and gain a clearer perspective.

I realize: *This is a VIPM (very important parenting moment). Releasing these feelings is so good for my child. This explosion will clear the air and lift my child's spirits. Staying present and calm, sticking with whatever limits I've set and being a safe channel for these emotions is the very best thing I could ever do.*

Some of the superhuman parenting powers my suit provides:

1. I understand that difficult behavior is a request for help — the best my child can do in that particular moment.

2. I remember to acknowledge my child's feelings and point-of-view. The importance of this can't be overemphasized.

3. I have the confidence to set and hold limits early (before I get annoyed or resentful) and do so calmly, directly, honestly, non-punitively.

4. I know that my words are often not enough. I must follow through by intervening to help my child stop the behavior.

5. I'm not afraid of what others think when I need to pick up and carry my crying, screaming child out of a problematic situation. My child comes first.

6. I have the courage to allow feelings to run their full course without trying to calm, rush, fix, shush, or talk my child out of them. I might say, "You have some very strong feelings about that," rather than yelling, "Enough!"

7. I move on without the slightest resentment once my child's storm has passed.

8. Rather than feeling angry, guilty, or dejected for the rest of the day, I hold my head high and congratulate myself for being an awesome, heroic parent.

Occasionally, though it's pretty rare, my superhero perspective even allows me to recognize the romance in these moments. I'm able to time travel at hyper-speed into the future, look back, and realize that this was prime time together. It didn't look pretty, but we were close. I'll remember how hard it was to love my child when she was at her very worst and feel super proud that I did it anyway.

14.

Why the Whining

A whining child, *my* child specifically, has got to be the most torturous sound I can imagine. I'd rather be trapped in a car with the alarm going off. It makes me feel intensely pressured to do something, to fix whatever it is *now*.

Getting our attention and unnerving us is what whining is supposed to do. If it's any consolation, just about every child goes through a whining phase (or two), and it's not indicative of a fatal flaw in our child or our parenting.

Here's how to help toddlers get what they need in a manner that's easier on our ears and nerves:

1. Don't let it rattle you. Some suggest ignoring behaviors like whining, but I believe in staying physically present and available, just disengaging from the whine.

Imagine yourself wearing an annoyance filter (an invention that could make billions, I'm sure). Take a deep breath and remind yourself that your child's behavior is perfectly normal, but that you don't want to encourage it. If we grant our child's request in order to stop the whining, or react negatively, we might do just that.

2. Gentle guidance. Calmly say something like, "It sounds like you're uncomfortable, but it's hard for me to understand you. Please tell me in your normal voice." You might add matter-of-factly, "That sound hurts my ears."

If the whining continues, return to whatever you might have been doing, and then after a moment try again. Or, you might ask the child some questions about what he wants while reminding him to answer in his normal voice.

3. Rest, food, drink, comfort. Whiners aren't functioning at their best, often as the result of not enough of these things. Remember, your toddlers are growing rapidly, tire easily, and have low blood sugar attacks before they realize they're hungry. They're also sprouting two-year molars, which is bound to create discomfort (and also interfere with sleep).

4. Whiners might be on the verge of an emotional explosion. Whining can be a sign that strong feelings of frustration, disappointment, sadness, or anger need to be expressed. If these feelings appear, welcome them, allow the feelings to run their course completely (in that moment and as a general rule), and the whining will likely cease.

5. Give undivided, positive attention. Even newborn babies know whether or not they have our full attention, and a day's worth of half-attention doesn't fulfill our child's needs. As Magda Gerber writes in *Your Self-Confident Baby*, our children need to periodically receive the message: "You are important. You are number one right now."

Magda encouraged parents to take advantage of feeding, bathing, diapering, and dressing as natural opportunities for one-on-one attention. She also recommended periods of "wants nothing" quality time; time when we allow our child to be the initiator of activities while we observe, support, respond, and participate *as the child requests*.

Unfortunately, no matter how much attention we give our children, they'll still try out whining when we aren't observing and listening to them. But if they don't get encouraging results, this too shall pass.

15.

Biting, Hitting, Kicking

We're big. They're tiny. They're just learning our rules and expectations for appropriate behavior. They have a developmental need to express their will, and they have very little (if any) impulse control. With these complicated, powerful dynamics in play, why would we take our toddler's hitting, biting, resistance, or refusal to cooperate personally?

We get triggered and become angry, frustrated, or scared. We might lose perspective and find ourselves stooping to our child's level, going at it head-to-head with a tot who's only a fraction of our size. We might be compelled to lash out, even hit or bite back(!), or attempt to regain control by sternly laying down the law, shaming or punishing our toddler in the name of *teaching a lesson.*

Or, perhaps we go the opposite direction. Fearful of confronting our child's rage or our own, we back down. We give in to our child, hesitate, waffle, or tippy-toe around the behavior. Perhaps we plead or cry so that our child feels sorry for us.

While these responses might seem effective in dealing with undesirable behavior in the moment, they end up making matters worse. Our intensity (which is always very apparent to children, so don't ever think they don't feel it) can turn a momentary experiment or impulsive act into a chronic behavioral issue. Children sense it when the leaders they count on have lost control, and that makes them feel less safe and too powerful. Punishments create fear, resentment, and distrust. Alternatively, our reluctance to set a definitive boundary also causes discomfort, insecurity, and more testing. Our vulnerability creates guilt.

Ultimately, these responses fail because they don't address the need all children are expressing through their misbehavior: *Help.*

When young children act out, they need our help. It's as simple as that. But how do we help them?

Perspective and attitude. If we can perceive our child's unpleasant actions as a young one's request for help, our role and our response become much clearer. As experienced, mature adults, this means rising above the fray (rather than getting caught in it) and providing assistance.

When we remind ourselves repeatedly that challenging behavior is a little lost child's distress call, we begin to see the ridiculousness of taking this behavior personally. We recognize the absurdity of reactions like "How could you treat me like this after all I do for you?! Why don't you listen?" Perspective gives us the patience, confidence, and the calm demeanor we need to be able to help.

Then we communicate and follow through: "You're having a hard time not hitting, so I will help by holding your hands." This is our thought process and might also be the words we say to our child.

Or we might say:

"I won't let you hit. You're so upset that I had to

put my phone away when you wanted to play with it. I know."

"I won't let you bite me. That hurts. I'm going to have to put you down and get something you can bite safely."

"Can you come indoors yourself or do you need my help? Looks like you need help, so I'm going to pick you up."

Anchors. We help our child and then allow for emotional explosions in response, because children need help with those, too. The assistance they need is an anchor — our patient presence and empathy while they safely ride this wave out. When the wave passes, they need us to acknowledge their feelings, forgive, understand, and let go so they can, too.

After all, how can we hold a grudge against a person whose impulses are bigger than they are?

This idea was brought home for me recently when walking down our hall at 10:45 PM to remind my teenager it was bedtime. I was startled to see my ten-year-old son (who had gone to sleep at 9 PM) striding towards me. First I thought he might be headed to the bathroom, but then he said something I couldn't make out: "Mumble, mumble... watch TV."

"What?" It then hit me that he was sleepwalking. For as long as any of us remember, he's had a nightly ritual of talking or shouting in his sleep, much to the amusement of his sisters who sleep in adjacent rooms. He often sits up in bed while spouting a phrase or two, but only occasionally does he embark on a nighttime stroll.

"Give me watch TV," he said again. This time I understood... sort of. He looked bewildered and deadpanned, "That makes no sense." Then he lurched toward the stairs.

"Ohhhh, no...you're going back to bed." He fought me while I tried to hold him off. We tussled. He's a strong, muscular little guy, a hardy opponent even in his sleep, but I finally managed to wrestle him back to his room and onto his bed where he was immediately calm and quiet again.

So, what does a ten-year-old sleepwalker have to do with a toddler acting out?

Toddlers are very conscious and aware, but their behavior *isn't*. They have about as much self-control as my boy does when he's sleepwalking, and like my son, they need us to handle their escapades confidently without getting angry.

Unruffled responses. A mom I've had the pleasure of consulting with over the phone recently shared her appreciation for the word I described previously in Chapter 12: *unruffled*. This mom thinks "unruffled" whenever her toddler's behavior challenges her. Since she had a new baby and her toddler needed to adjust to this tremendous change in his life, she needed to imagine unruffled a lot. She doesn't so much anymore, however, because her unruffled responses have helped her boy pass through this difficult stage quickly.

We can't fake unruffled. Like good actors, parents have to *believe*. We acquire this belief when we maintain a realistic perspective and adopt the attitude that we're big and on top of things, our child is little, and discipline equals help.

Another mom's note made me smile:

Dear Janet:

My 16-month-old son Jamie has taken to hitting – hitting me, specifically. He seems to be acting out of pure joy. Meaning, he isn't hungry, tired, or frustrated. On the contrary, he seems thrilled by the exclamation "Ow!" and wants to provoke it. He cheerfully chirps "Ow! Ow! Ow!" as he tries to punch me in the face, smiling and laughing the entire time. A part of me finds it adorable.

So far I have tried many times: "I'm not going to let you do that" and "no," and gently stopped his hands. Also I blank my face so I'm not smiling back, but I'm not getting emotional or upset.

He probably hasn't developed empathy yet, but he is still repeatedly hitting me and now trying it on our 19-year-old cat.

Plus, he got me in the eye last week – it's challenging to not be upset when it hurts. Any advice?

Like many perceptive toddlers, Jamie is as acutely aware of a subpar performance as a mini Roger Ebert. He's not buying the blank face. He heard "Ow!" once, and that's all he needed. He knows there are more still in there somewhere. He's getting to his mom, and it's exciting.

Jennifer has to *believe* this is not a big deal at all. She has to think *booooring* while she gently but firmly stops Jamie from hitting her. She has to rise way above this being a serious problem and perceive her little guy's behavior as totally nonthreatening for it to cease. Right now, she's getting caught up in the drama a bit (which is admittedly hard not to do with such a captivating toddler).

The beauty of an unruffled, helpful attitude is that

it allows our child to relax knowing his parents 'have his back'. He knows we won't get too flustered by his mischief. He's assured he has anchors — patient teachers capable of handling anything he tosses their way with relative ease.

With the knowledge that their parents will always help them handle the behaviors they can't handle themselves, children feel safe to struggle, make mistakes, grow, and learn with confidence.

"Toddlers test limits to find out about themselves and other people. By stopping children in a firm, but respectful way when they push our limits, we're helping them to figure out their world and to feel safe."

　　　- Irene Van der Zande, *1, 2, 3…The Toddler Years*

16.

Food Fight

Most parents realize that a healthy diet is essential to their toddler's overall well-being and make it a priority to provide regular, nutritious meals. But, for any number of reasons, our toddlers don't always show their appreciation for our hard work and good intentions.

It's difficult not to feel like a failure if our child won't eat. It's also difficult not to take it personally. The more we persist, however, the more our child resists.

Hi Janet,

I'm hoping you can help my wife and me with some advice in regards to some recent food issues with our 18-month-old daughter, Tessa.

When we put her on solids a little over a year ago, she took to them with fervor. She ate up everything. My wife worked like crazy and made all of the baby food ground up from organic veggies. Tessa loved everything. Eventually, we added turkey meat, eggs and other foods. Tessa continued to like everything.

In recent months, Tessa's not eating as much, and she is incredibly picky. We're wondering what happened to that little girl who devoured everything at all her meals. Today for lunch, I made her scrambled eggs with green beans and cheese. Eggs were always one of her favorites. Today, she tried a few pieces and immediately spit it out. I waited and kept encouraging her to eat and telling her she likes eggs. After playing with them for about five minutes, she put another piece in her mouth, which she immediately spit out, and then cleared her entire tray of food onto the floor.

Our mealtimes are increasingly becoming this type of battle, and it's wearing on me and my wife. We spent a week in Portland last week and every meal out was a nightmare. We ended up getting take-out food and eating in our hotel room.

I thought teething was the issue for a while so I was willing to give Tessa a break and offer different foods, but now I'm worried this is going to become a habit and I'm hoping for some help.

Thanks, Janet!
Chris

Dear Chris:

I love toddlers. Open, aware, sensitive, intuitive, they've had us pegged since their first weeks in our arms, and we now begin to discover how truly brilliant they are.

First, as I imagine you've done already, rule out any possible medical issues by checking with your doctor, especially if Tessa is losing weight or not gaining properly. But even if she does have a digestive issue of some kind, the family goal is for mealtimes to revert back to being a peaceful, comfortable time to focus on eating and each other rather than a battleground. Here's what I'm guessing may have happened...

Blessed with doting parents who value healthy food and "worked like crazy" to give her la crème de la crème from her very first mouthful, Tessa responded beautifully and rewarded her parents' efforts by eating with gusto. At mealtime, the family was not only refueled by delicious food, it was an unadulterated success for everyone. Happy times.

Then something happened. Your guess is as good (or better) than mine: teething; a cold; a change of taste; or just a period of growth when Tessa didn't have her usual appetite. Children go through phases when they eat less.

This change in Tessa's eating caused her parents a teensy weensy bit of concern, and her antenna picked up a vibe (with a toddler's sixth sense, it doesn't take much). She felt some tension surrounding her and food.

At the same time, because she is secure in her parents' love, Tessa is beginning to explore some areas of interest two-year-olds are fond of: testing, independence, power, control, will. Fun stuff. This stage of development is trying for parents. It takes practice to find the healthy balance of power with a toddler, but resisting her parents and asserting herself is exactly what Tessa should be doing. She's right on track.

Eating is an area Tessa controls and *needs* to control. She is the only one who knows when she's hungry and when she's full. She has to listen to her tummy and trust herself. Lately, mealtime has become a little too "loaded" for her to be able to listen. She's not trying to torture you; she's just feeling her power and playing her role, which is to resist anything she perceives as pressure.

Here are my suggestions for a truce:

Don't invest or anticipate. Lower your expectations about mealtimes with Tessa. (After your recent experiences, this probably goes without saying!) This isn't the time for you or your wife to prepare meals for Tessa à la Mario Batali and set yourselves up for feeling disappointed and unappreciated. Do that when it's just the two of you, but for Tessa keep it simple.

Since you're human, you may be projecting your anticipation (or even dread) of a scene at mealtime without realizing it. When we've been dealing with weeks of resistance from our children, whether it's about eating, diaper changes, going to bed, or whatever, we can't help but project trepidation, which can make matters worse. Since toddlers sense our feelings, wiping the slate clean and projecting confidence and calmness works best. Likewise it helps to...

Temper reactions and responses. Be aware of subtext. Make eating solely about the relationship between Tessa and her tummy. Don't get excited when she eats well, disappointed when she doesn't, coax or encourage her. For now and the future, be careful not to give Tessa the impression that the amount she eats pleases or even affects mom, dad, or anyone.

Instead, encourage her to focus on her physical needs — her appetite and sense of fullness — by staying neutral. This requires tempering feelings, curbing both enthusiasm and worry. Since our toddlers are very, very, very smart and can read between the lines, we can't even give them the gentle reminder that they like eggs without them sensing our agenda. Believe it.

I've had parents in my classes with underweight toddlers — one mom who was even told that her child had *failure to thrive*. Imagine how challenging it was to stay neutral when food was presented and not worry. Another mom realized it worked best to leave the room and let her toddler eat meals with just her older sister whenever possible until the toddler gained enough weight for the mom to be able to stop projecting tension. I'm not suggesting anyone do this, just illustrating the powerful effect we can have.

Give choices and small portions. Present less than you think Tessa will eat – very small amounts of 3 or 4 types of food. Keep the rest handy. Let her eat as much or as little as she wishes and be the one to ask for more. What she chooses and how much she swallows has to be in her control.

Be sure to let her know that when she signals she is done — slows down, starts fiddling with food, or (ahem) throwing it down — mealtime is over, and she won't have another opportunity to eat until the next meal or snack. This isn't punitive. It's giving her the autonomy, choices, limits, and consequences she needs.

Try not to get angry or annoyed if she acts out with food. Keep your cool and say something like "Hmmm. You're spitting. You must be telling me you're done." Then follow through with conviction by taking the food away and kindly helping her out of her chair, always telling Tessa what you are doing.

Switching out a highchair for a toddler-sized table and chair or stool works wonders to eliminate eating battles. (For details and a brief video demonstration, please see "Babies With Table Manners" on my website.)

Let go and trust. Channeling Marianne Williamson: 'trusting' and 'letting go' are recurring themes for parents, too, and it's always a struggle to figure out how and when to do it. Toddlers sometimes lose their appetites when they feel pressured around eating, but they do not go on hunger strikes. Project trust, be okay with it even if Tessa skips a few meals, and she'll be back to normal again soon, and onto testing elsewhere.

Bon appétit!

17.

Sassy, Bossy Back-Talk

Hi Janet,

I am having a tough time with my almost two-and-a-half-year-old daughter, Madeline. I have practiced RIE since before she was born while I worked in infant care, so your approach is what I am used to around children. She has thus far been brought up in a very calm, patient, encouraging, respectful home.

Madeline has always been an easy-going child – very empathetic, happy, independent ... all around great. Recently, she has started to "back-talk," and apparently it is the button to push! When I (or my husband) am trying to tell her something, she argues with us to the point where I don't really know where to go before it turns into an argument or power struggle. For example:

Grampie was in the bathroom and she was standing at the closed door yelling for him. I told her, "Madeline, Grampie is just going to the washroom. He will be out soon. He needs some privacy. Please stop shouting at him." She started shouting back to me "No! No, he doesn't need his privacy!"

She hit me with a toy (half-by-accident, I think...), and I told her "Ouch! That hurts me. I don't like it." She replied (quite indignantly), "Yeah, ya do!" This happens quite often when I express my own feelings to her – she replies, with lots of attitude, the opposite.

I understand that it is a time of independence and she is

learning how to be her own person. I understand that it is a very conflicting and confusing time for her because she wants to be independent but still needs us. We have always given her lots of space and time and choices, so this is new for us. I don't really know what to do.

Lisa

Hi, Lisa:

You nailed the issue here: "She has started to 'back-talk,' and apparently it is the button to push!" Madeline continues to push your button because it works — the back-talk is getting a rise out of you. The solution may be very simple: deactivate this button so the behavior loses its power.

I realize that this might not be as easy as it sounds. It may not even seem right to you. Yes, this is rude behavior, and if anyone other than your own 2.5-year-old daughter treated you this way, you'd be rightfully offended. And, of course, the fact that this *is* your empathetic, all-around-great little girl whom you've adored and respected makes it feel a million times worse. It's surprising and alarming. How dare she? What's happening to your precious girl? Where is this obnoxious behavior coming from, and how do we put a stop to it?

If you were a less empathetic, knowledgeable parent, you'd probably spank her or put her in time-out; but since you are respectful and enlightened, I advise something far more effective: **adjust your perspective**.

There is surely some good news here, so focus on that. Consider this:

1. As you know, toddlers need to test their power,

express their individuality, try stuff out. Madeline's right on track.

2. Toddlers commonly express their burgeoning independence by disagreeing with us, no matter what it's about. Magda Gerber used to tell the story of a toddler shouting "no" before eagerly accepting an ice-cream cone from her parent.

Defiance is an almost automatic response, so when we say "yes," toddlers have an *overpowering* compulsion to say "no" (and vice-versa), whether or not they really mean it. It's nothing personal.

3. Madeline is talking!

4. She has strong opinions and the attitude to go with them, some of which are going to be nutty and inappropriate. But the fact that she expresses herself this way means she's an assertive, self-confident girl.

5. I'm usually not one to compare young children to animals, but when I think of toddlers experimenting with their power, I see gorillas beating their chests. Woo-hoo! It's a powerful time.

6. She's testing these behaviors out at home where she knows she's safe, loved, and generally accepted, which means you've nurtured her well.

7. She's tiny and 2.5 years old. I imagine you and your husband are quite a bit taller and at least... 20 years old? In other words, don't take Madeline's hollering and back-talk personally or feel the slightest bit threatened by your blustery little girl. See this for the healthy testing it is, and rise above it.

Here are some "Take Two" suggestions for the Grampie-in-the-washroom example you gave me:

It sounds like you began to get a little wound up when Madeline was hustling poor Grampie out of the washroom, but you tried to keep your cool. How was your tone, do you think? Did you seem calm and unfazed?

Take a step back. Isn't it kind of sweet that this commanding little toddler wants her Grampie so badly and thinks she might be powerful enough to eject him from the washroom? I know *I'd* be flattered if that were my grandchild. So, if I were you, I would say lightly, "Somebody really wants her Grampie! Madeline, I think Grampie may have heard you... and he might need another minute or two." I'd leave it at that.

Besides, can't Grampie fend for himself?

When Madeline hit you with the toy (which probably wouldn't have happened if she hadn't sensed you were upset about Grampie), your response set you up for even more button-pushing. Stopping her before she hit you would have been ideal. "Ouch!" is fine, and "that hurts me" is okay if you aren't too emotional about it. But you might have taken the behavior a little too personally when you added, "I don't like it."

Believe it or not, these few extra words could have been enough to indicate to Madeline that this minor incident had the power to upset you, when what she needed was reassurance that you were confidently in charge. So, she continued her button-pushing barrage with her pugnacious response, "Yeah, ya do!"

When children do this it's as if they're saying,

"Can you handle this? Can you handle me? Please prove that you can handle me with ease."

Here are some other light-hearted (but not sarcastic), deactivating responses to bossiness and back-talk:

"Well, I guess we disagree on *that* one."

"Hmm... Thank you for your opinion."

"You seem to have strong feelings about (Grampie leaving the washroom, etc.)"

And when in doubt, there's always, "Interesting!"

So, take a step back, react and worry less, and enjoy your daughter's spirit!

18.

Stop Feeling Threatened

When I consult with parents about their children's more challenging behaviors, I sometimes offer a visual that I hope will put otherwise volatile situations into perspective. I've been reluctant to share this on my website for fear it might be misinterpreted, but since so many of the parents I hear from continue to struggle with remaining centered and calm when their children push limits and buttons, I decided to risk it and share my descriptor: *teddy bear behavior*.

I know — teddy bears are objects; babies definitely are not. I'll explain, but first a bit of context...

Our children are born sentient, as present as you and me, and so our primary job is forging person-to-person relationships with them — relationships that are honest, caring, respectful, and unconditionally loving.

Yet all children exhibit behaviors that are impulsive and irrational, especially during periods in their development when they need to resist us in order to test their wings (like the toddler and teen years). How are we supposed to respect our small "person" when she can be so disrespectful, hurtful, and downright rude?

Some might conclude that young children are

nothing more than thoughtless beasts (and that would explain the "taming your toddler" type of advice, which includes distractions, tricks, treats, and other manipulative interventions). It's easy to get personally offended or fear that we've failed our child somehow, that we didn't teach her appropriate behavior or respect.

Triggered by our anger, frustration, fear, or guilt, we are likely to respond in a manner that unfortunately creates even more challenging behavior. Truly, when children repeatedly test, it is more often than not the *direct result* of our previous responses. That is why remaining calm and centered matters. A lot.

The easiest and surest way to calm ourselves is perspective, which might mean reminding ourselves that the toddler screaming and swinging at us is a tiny person who has spent only two and a half years on this planet. She needs us to tolerate her screams and stop her from hitting, but a response of anger or confusion would be unsettling to her, to say the least.

And so I suggest that parents suffering the slings and arrows of a child's behavior consider it in the context of something cuddly and benign, like a teddy bear.

Teddy bear behavior includes occasional hitting, kicking, biting, screaming, whining, refusing to follow directions, resistance, rejection, "I hate you" (in all its forms), and grumpy teenagers scrutinizing you under a microscope and criticizing every single thing you say, do, and wear. It is age-appropriate and can certainly be annoying, but it is essentially harmless. If we can perceive teddy bear behavior for what it is and respond appropriately, it will be temporary and not progress to chronic, dangerous, or harmful.

Teddy bear behavior is sparked by:
- A need for the reassurance our gentle leadership provides
- Stress, hunger, exhaustion
- Fear, sadness, anger, frustration — all of which children need us to help them express
- Feeling out of favor, ignored, unloved
- Emotions surrounding transitions: the addition of a sibling, moving to a new home, attending school for the first time, changing schools, changes of any kind
- Developmental phases and milestones
- The two's and teenage years are classic teddy bear territory, but ages four, six, and early adolescence (ages nine and up) can also be teddy bear periods.

Teddy bear behavior is eased when we:
- Feel unthreatened, breathe, project confidence, let it rollll off our back
- Prevent it whenever possible (by giving children safe "yes" places to explore; for example, rather than free access to markers and white sofas)
- Set limits calmly, clearly, early
- Acknowledge all desires and feelings and encourage children to express them ("You feel like throwing the trucks. I can't let you. That's unsafe. Are you upset about Daddy leaving for work? You sometimes miss him

> when he goes. Over there are some safe
> toys you can throw.")

- Discern needs and do our best to meet them

Perceiving teddy bear behavior doesn't ever mean *treating* children like teddy bears, objectifying them, ignoring them, or talking down to them with patronizing words and cutesy voices. Children are whole people who always deserve our respect and authenticity.

However, once teddy bear behavior has subsided, they might want a cuddle, whatever their age.

19.

Don't Fight the Feelings

One of the most ironically counterintuitive twists of parenting is this: the more we welcome our children's displeasure, the happier everyone in our household will be.

There is no greater gift to our children and ourselves than complete acceptance of their negative feelings. (Notice, I did not say "behaviors".) By deleting from our parenting job description the responsibilities to 'soothe', 'correct', and 'control' our kids' feelings and replacing them with 'accept', 'acknowledge', and 'support', both parent and child are rewarded and liberated.

It can be intensely challenging to let go of our own reactiveness and patiently allow our children to feel. With practice, however, it gets easier. It is the key to:

- Successful limit setting
- Fewer battles, more peace
- Our child's emotional health and healing
- Mutual trust
- A strong bond
- Resilient, secure, authentic kids

Jennifer allowed me to share this note about her

personal "victory":

Hello Janet!

I want to say thank you for being out there. I found your blog a couple of months ago. All difficult questions about parenting being so close to me, your advice and notes were such a treasure.

My son is 7, my daughter is 2. I have major issues with my son. I often used guilt to get something from him, and now it shows. It was easy to intimidate a little child, but it doesn't work with a 7-year-old. I tried many different ways and styles, but nothing seemed just right... And here is your blog, and at last I felt I found what is needed!

My favorite book always was "Children Are From Heaven" by John Gray. I loved everything about it, except time-outs. They seemed somehow wrong to me, but I didn't know what to do instead. It is cowardly to deal with a child's tantrum this way, to just put him in his room and close the door... But it never crossed my mind to just be right near him, sitting with him during the storm. My son would explode for every small reason and accuse me about everything and throw harsh words at me. I was instantly triggered and involved, and there we'd be, standing against each other, screaming and accusing... Time-outs seemed much better to me.

And now I'm trying everything you are writing about, and today was the first big victory! Not over my son, but over myself.

Today I was calm, and I was able to stay calm all the way through the tantrum. I was just listening to his harsh words and kept repeating that he was tired and angry because I would not let him watch cartoons. I assured him that feeling angry was ok. When he tried throwing things or to hit, I held him and said that I won't let him do it.

It was lasting forever... But I just stayed calm, did not

answer his accusations and stayed with him.

The interesting thing was that my daughter usually hates it when we fight, but this time she was calm and just played near us like nothing was happening! And just when I thought that this was not working, my son embraced me and said, "I'm so sorry mom, I don't want to fight anymore, forgive me please!"

I won that battle against myself, and now it will be easier. I know that it works, and I know what to do. It was not easy, but it was worth it.

Thank you so much, Janet! My son is not a toddler, but I hope I can overcome that harm I did in the past... We are blessed with such people like you, thank you for being there!

Sincerely,
Jennifer

20.

The Healing Power of Tantrums

The madness began at snack time, which we offer in our RIE parenting classes once the babies are all mobile and able to sit independently. Participation in snack time is always the children's choice, and they quickly learn and enjoy the routine.

They are requested to sit on the floor at the snack table (or on stools once they're walking and able to sit at a slightly higher table). We ask them to wipe their hands, choose bibs, eat as much or as little of the snack (bananas) as they wish, and remain seated until *they* decide they are done. We gently, but assuredly prevent them from leaving the table with food. (*Babies With Table Manners* on YouTube provides an example.)

The children in this class were 12-13 months, and we'd been doing snack somewhat successfully for about six weeks. But on that day, there must have something in the air, because all the toddlers were testing me like crazy — sitting down and then popping up again, climbing on the table. It was a mutiny.

Lily's testing was especially forceful and persistent, which was surprisingly out of character. She had always been a remarkably peaceful, mild, and graceful baby.

Again and again Lily climbed onto the table and had to be helped down. Offering her the option to "get down by yourself" quickly became pointless, because she was clearly 'out of herself' and possessed by some fervent agenda.

"You want to climb on the table, but I can't let you. I'm going to help you down," I repeated…repeatedly.

Finally, Lily's mom asked if she should come and help me, because it was impossible for me to assist the other children while Lily kept popping onto the table.

I could see Lily's mom was perplexed and concerned. "Hmmm…maybe she's confused because at home she sits on a stool next to her sister," she suggested.

Suddenly doubting myself, I considered this for a moment. Could she be confusing the table for a stool? It didn't seem possible. Lily's way too smart for that.

As Lily's mom took over and was stopping her from climbing on the table, Lily became increasingly upset, started yelling, crying, having a total meltdown. I could see how this rattled her mom. I asked her, "Has she ever acted this way before?" She said no and looked worried. I sensed she thought that Lily really wanted something to eat and was maybe hoping I would change the rules of our routine to make it work for her. The thought of doing so certainly crossed my mind. I was seriously questioning myself.

After five minutes or so of intense crying and struggling, Lily finally calmed down, sat with her mom for a bit, and then started playing again, never having eaten a bite of banana.

Although Lily seemed fine, I was still uncomfortable because I knew Lily's mom was disturbed by this episode. Then a few minutes later she realized: "We've had family staying with us for the last five weeks...and it's been fun, but disruptive and stressful. Maybe..."

Ah-ha! So perhaps sweet, gentle Lily had some overpowering feelings stuck inside her that she needed to release, and RIE's therapeutic "all feelings welcome" environment plus our patient, persistent limit-holding was what allowed her to do it.

Young children are self-healing geniuses. Have you noticed? Sometimes their tantrums are an expression of immediate discomfort like fatigue or hunger. Other times, however, they have a backlog of internalized feelings and will seem to deliberately and (seemingly) unreasonably push our limits so that we will hold steady and resist, which then opens up the escape valve they need to release these emotions. But this process can only work for them when we are able to set and hold limits and bravely accept their feelings.

Experiences like Lily's profoundly reiterate for me that we must trust our children's self-healing abilities and know that every one of their feelings is absolutely perfect.

The following week in class Lily did something else she'd never done before. As soon as she entered the classroom, she crawled straight over to me and put her head in my lap. After our debacle the week before, she seemed to be saying 'thanks' or 'sorry', but I really think it was thanks.

21.

Your Child's New Baby Blues

I'd just landed at LAX and was waiting at the baggage claim carousel when I heard an angry exchange. I turned toward the adjacent carousel and saw a three or four-year-old girl decked out in a colorful traveling ensemble – brightly patterned leggings, a trendy t-shirt, and pink plastic movie star sunglasses. She seemed to be fumbling for something in her polka dot backpack while her father glared at her and seethed, "Just *be nice*. Be nice to your sister!"

Several feet away stood her mother, who also glared as she held baby sister (about 12 months old) in her arms. The girl kept her composure but avoided her parents' gaze. She seemed alone and vulnerable, a "problem child" estranged from her family.

If this mini-snapshot was typical of her family dynamic, it was hard to fathom this little girl ever feeling anything other than resentment towards her baby sister.

There is nothing that rocks a toddler's world like the arrival, or impending arrival, of a new sibling. The changes this event causes within a family's dynamic — no matter how aware, sensitive, and caring the parents may be — are always deeply registered by its youngest, most vulnerable, and sensitive member. It can cause all sorts of behavioral changes, including developmental regression, mood swings, and severe testing.

When I consult with a parent about a sudden or extreme behavioral issue in a toddler, I ask a lot of questions and play detective, learning all I can about the toddler in question and the family dynamics. Often, at some point I just have to ask (suspecting I already know the answer): "Have there been any major changes in the past few weeks or months?"

On more occasions than I can count, the answer is: "Well, we *do* have a new baby…," or "I'm in my third trimester…"

Here are some key points to keep in mind during this difficult adjustment:

1. Have reasonable expectations. No matter how much the older child may have wished for a baby brother or sister, the reality of this shift in the parents' attention and affection is felt as a loss. Children often feel grief, sadness and sometimes anger or guilt, but mostly they are fearful of losing their parents' love.

Overwhelmed by this tumultuous blend of emotions, which are nearly impossible for children to understand (much less articulate), they act out their pain through irritating behaviors that are sometimes aggressive. Mood swings can be extreme.

Parents might be shocked to discover an unpleasant side to their child they hadn't known existed, especially if they expected her to be a loving, adoring, and helpful big sister during this adjustment. These behaviors are bound to push parents' buttons, yet since the child is experiencing an emotional crisis, she needs the assurance of her parents' love and empathy now more than ever.

2. Encourage children to express feelings. There are a couple of important ways parents can help children express their feelings in a healthy manner:

a) When children act out with the baby — kissing or patting the baby too hard or jumping on the bed next to her — after calmly but confidently stating the boundary ("I can't let you..."), the parent can ask matter-of-factly, "Are you feeling rough toward the baby right now? Are you upset that the baby's here? Big sisters often feel that way. But I'm going to help you get down from the bed. I'd love for you to sit on my lap or jump on the floor next to me."

b) Casually bring up the subject of negative feelings as often as possible: "Being a big sister is very hard sometimes. It's normal to get angry at the baby or at mom or dad, feel sad, worry or just be upset and not know why. If you feel any of those things I want to know. I will *always* understand, love you, and want to help you."

It may feel counterintuitive to suggest these feelings to your child (won't this *encourage* her to feel negatively toward the baby?). The truth is that the more you can openly accept and acknowledge, even welcome your child's negative thoughts and emotions, the more space you will clear for her to form a genuinely loving bond with her sibling.

3. But why mention negatives when my child seems fine? Some children do seem to adapt to life with the new baby peacefully. Why would we project about problems that don't exist?

It is my view that the children who seem more accepting and tolerant of this huge life change need even more encouragement to express negative feelings than those who overtly struggle. No matter how positive any change is, there are also elements of fear and loss. *For all of us.* If these feelings aren't addressed and expressed, they are internalized. You may have a well-behaved child, but chances are good she's suffering inside.

4. Avoid guilt-inducing comments. When parents are expecting baby number two, friends and relatives will often comment to the firstborn child, "Ooh, bet you can't *wait* to be a big sister!" But by then it's already begun to dawn on the older child that 'big sister' isn't all it's cracked up to be. They've sensed that the focus of everyone's attention has shifted away from them. Their future feels uncertain, and it will only get worse. They need someone who understands their pain and can assure them that their mixed feelings (especially the negative ones) are perfectly valid, or they are likely to turn these feelings inward.

5. Don't judge. Again, this is about adjusting our expectations and understanding that button-pushing behaviors are the manifestation of our child's pain and confusion.

When we label a behavior "not nice," "mean," or "bad," children take these judgments personally. It's not only the behavior that's bad — *they* are bad. When the people they trust and need most in the world tell them they are "not nice," they believe it, and this rejection is profound.

6. Lessen tension by not sweating the small stuff. Second children are born into a much different environment than their big brothers and sisters. Having an older sibling is exciting. So, as much as possible, let it be. Let it be noisier and more chaotic, and let there be more interruptions to the baby's playtime. Let big sister take toys away from the baby when they're "playing together" as long as this is physically safe. Understand that this impulse is powerful and symbolic of the rivalry the older child feels.

Most babies don't mind the toys being removed from them unless their parents do. In fact, this is the way they play with another child. The less you focus on these harmless behaviors, the less compelling it will be for the older child to repeat them.

7. Understand your child's need for trust and autonomy. Ask for her help whenever possible, especially regarding the baby's care. When children's emotions are out of control, opportunities to feel autonomous have a calming effect. But don't be disappointed if your child turns you down, because saying "no" is also a way for her to feel autonomous.

8. One-on-one time. Periods of time alone with your children are a necessity. For both the baby and the older child, it's about quality, not quantity.

Set aside at least 20 minutes a day in which you are wholly present and focused on your older child (which might mean aiming toward giving the baby an earlier bedtime). Then, when you need to focus on the baby and your child struggles, you can calmly acknowledge, "I see how uncomfortable it is for you when I am feeding the baby. That is really hard for you, I know. I'm so looking forward to our time together tonight after the baby goes to bed. Think about what you'd like to do together."

9. Foster the baby's independent play. A baby who can self-entertain is even more of a blessing the second time around, because his or her independent play creates opportunities for parents to be available to the older child without the baby always between them.

Provide a safe, enclosed play space (a crib or playpen is fine for the first months) so that the baby doesn't need constant supervision. Your toddler will probably need this boundary, because the impulse to test the parents by bothering the baby can be strong.

10. Respect your children's continued need for boundaries and calm, helpful parents who are on their side. Although extreme exhaustion or guilt might lead us to ease up on boundaries during this period of transition and emotional turmoil, our children need the love and security of our limits now more than ever.

They'll need us to give them matter-of-fact reminders like "I don't want you to touch the baby when you are in a jumpy mood"; choices like "You can stay next to me quietly while I put the baby to bed, or play in the next room." Sometimes they'll need us to follow through by gently but firmly physically containing them or removing them from situations.

Most crucially, they'll need us to intervene way before we lose our temper or think they're "not nice" — and with all the confidence, calmness, patience, and empathy we can muster.

22.

Common Discipline Mistakes

Disclaimer: In the diverse and sometimes divisive world of parenting advice, one parent's mistake is another's best practice.

So, for clarification, the way I define 'mistake' reflects the parenting goals I personally aspire to and is based on my experiences working with parents and toddlers for the last 20 years. I consider these mistakes because whether or not they might seem to work in the moment, they can undermine the ultimate goal most of us have — a loving, trusting relationship with our child.

The word 'discipline' is a mistake in itself, because for most of us it connotes punishment, and according to *The Oxford Dictionary*'s first definition, the two go hand-in-hand: *"The practice of training people to obey rules or a code of behavior, using punishment to correct disobedience."*

Since I consider punishment the biggest discipline mistake of all, I'm ditching Oxford's meaning and going with the definition Magda Gerber shares in *Dear Parent: Caring for Infants With Respect*: "Training that develops self-control, character."

This is more in line with the actual source of the

word, the Latin *disciplina,* which means "instruction, knowledge."

So, discipline is educating our children to understand appropriate behavior, values, and how to control their impulses. Here are some teaching methods and misconceptions that either *mis*-educate or just get in the way:

Punishments. There are several reasons punishments (including spanking, time-out, and "consequences" when presented punitively) are mistakes. The most crucial is that children who are taught through physical or emotional pain tend to stop trusting us and themselves. Expecting humans at their most vulnerable stage of life to learn through pain and shame (when healthy adults would never put up with this) doesn't make a lot of sense, does it? Can you imagine taking a college course and being spanked or banished to time-out because you weren't learning quickly enough?

Even if punishments didn't have long-term negative effects, the truth is they don't work. The loving, trusting bond our children have with us is what makes following our code of behavior and internalizing our values something they *want* to do. Erode that relationship, and discipline becomes an us-against-them struggle.

Perceiving children as "bad" rather than in need of help. There was a child in one of my parent/toddler guidance classes whose behavior could be considered "bad". He was compelled to push limits, probably because his adoring, gentle mother struggled to set them confidently. She admitted that his behavior unnerved her. That, in turn, unnerved him, and acting out was the way he demonstrated it.

Some days I would have to calmly follow this boy, shadowing him so that he wouldn't push or tackle one of the other 18–24-month-olds. When I sensed an aggressive impulse coming, I would place my hand in the way and say matter-of-factly, "I won't let you push," or gently move him away from the friend he was tackling and say, "That's too rough."

There was no point in reminding him to touch gently (in fact, that would have been an insult to his intelligence). He knew *exactly* what 'gentle' meant and was clearly making a different choice.

But what I *would* often end up asking was "Are you having a hard time today?"

"Da," he'd answer a bit wistfully, a hint of a smile on his face and recognition in his eyes. This simple acknowledgement coupled with my calm, consistent limit setting would usually ease the behavior.

Toddlers love to be understood. They also need to know that their discipline teachers are calm, unruffled, and understanding, not thrown or upset by their behavior.

And that is the way that I have come to understand misbehavior. It is not intentionally bad, mean, or a way to upset parents. It is a request for help.

Help me, I'm tired.
Help me, I have low blood sugar.
Help me stop hitting my friends.
Help me stop annoying or angering you.
(Better yet, stop me before I do those things.)
Help me by remaining calm so I sense how capable you

are at taking care of me.

Help me by empathizing, so that I know you understand and still love me.

Help me so that I can let go of these urges and distractions and be playful, joyful, and free again.

23.

Setting Limits Without Yelling

In the last chapter I explained why punishments and the perception of children misbehaving as "bad" undermine effective and respectful discipline.

In the following email exchange, I discuss with Lauren (mother to a toddler) some other common discipline missteps:

- Yelling
- Not setting limits early enough (which often leads to yelling or at least feeling like yelling)
- Not following through (which can also lead to yelling)

Dear Janet,

I've been a reader for about a year, and I've found the tenets of RIE to be indispensable with my daughter. I'm a SAHM (stay-at-home-mom), and it's incredible how much better our days go when I'm able to maintain a calm face and tone when setting limits.

My problem is that I'm not very good at it. Sometimes I just get so frustrated with the constant demands of a 2.5 year old that I end up yelling.

My question is whether you have any advice about how

to stay calm and consistent. I'm already very much a believer, but I need something to help me manage my frustration level in the moment.

While I know it's absolutely unreasonable to expect my daughter to know when she's pushed enough, I can't help wanting to say something like, "Come on, kid, I've nailed the respectful-but-firm tone here a few times already, and now I'm not screwing around!"

The thing is, when it works, which is a lot of the time, it really works. It seems like that would be enough incentive for me, but I still struggle. I'm sure if I were to get this question from another parent, I'd know exactly what to tell them, yet putting it into practice consistently when the going gets tough is not easy for me. Any hot tips?

Thank you so much,

Lauren

Hi, Lauren:

Two and a half is a demanding age, but "constant demands" was a clue for me that there is something in the dynamic between you and your daughter that is unsettling her. There shouldn't be constant demands. But if she senses that she is pushing your buttons and that there might be an explosion (yelling and frustration on your part, etc.), then she is going to be compelled to make more demands.

In haste,

Janet

Thanks, Janet. She definitely can sense when she's pushing my buttons, that's very true. I don't think I made a fair characterization of the situation by describing her demands as constant.

She really is wonderful at self-entertaining, and we do

everything we can to foster her independence and follow her lead. For example, she has just learned to open the screen door herself. I think this is great, because we have a safe, fenced back yard, and she's able to spend as much time as she likes playing out there.

As an example of something that pushes my buttons, now that she can open the screen door, she sometimes gets in a spell of throwing things outside, and she won't stop until we lock the door. It doesn't matter what we say, whether we do the calm "I won't let you do that," she keeps doing it...she won't stop. The thing is, I don't want to lock the door as an artificial limit. I want her to just do what I say.

I guess my feeling is (and I know it's a completely unreasonable expectation) that I want her to understand how hard we work to be respectful parents, to give her as much freedom and autonomy as she can handle, and to give us the benefit of the doubt and respect when we do say "no". When she blatantly does something we've nicely told her she may not do, it feels hurtful and disrespectful to me, and I have a lot of difficultly not taking it personally.

What I'd love to be better at is just saying, after one warning, "I'm going to lock the door now because you're having a hard time keeping things in the house," and calmly getting up and doing it.

I think my problem, now that I'm talking it out, is that I give her too many chances, more than I can handle, to comply on her own. In my effort to give her the opportunity to choose to do what I'm asking of her, I end up pushing myself farther than I can handle.

So what's the best way to balance giving her a chance to decide and comply on her own without stepping in and enforcing the limit?

Hi, Lauren:

Yes! You answered your own question: *"What I'd*

love to be better at is just saying, after one warning, "I'm going to lock the door now because you're having a hard time keeping things in the house," and calmly getting up and doing it. I think my problem, now that I'm talking it out, is that I give her too many chances, more than I can handle, to comply on her own. In my effort to give her the opportunity to choose to do what I'm asking of her, I end up pushing myself farther than I can handle."

It seems that you are expecting too much of your toddler and misunderstanding why she is "misbehaving". Yes, she can understand what you want; but no, she can't just agree and quietly comply with your wishes out of respect. This isn't personal; it's developmental.

A vital part of her development right now is testing her power and her will, while also being assured that she has parents who are well-equipped to contain this power. Toddlers do this by resisting us. They can't explore their will by saying, "Yes, mom, I'll do what you ask." So, defiance at this age is normal and healthy.

However, it is disconcerting and even scary for toddlers to feel too powerful – powerful enough to push parents' buttons and rattle or anger them, or powerful enough to make decisions they can't easily make (like when to relinquish their will, follow a parent's direction and stop throwing toys). Feeling too powerful means feeling uncared for, and toddlers are acutely aware of their need for our care.

Your daughter wants and needs you to follow through and lock the door. Then, if she has feelings about that, allow and acknowledge them. She needs you to calmly connect and "parent her" *way before* you get angry. If you are getting annoyed, that means you are giving her too many chances and choices. She's clearly letting you know that she needs your help.

My thought is that she may also be communicating that she's tired, hungry, or in need of release for some pent up feelings. But one thing is certain: she is asking for a boundary from you, presented calmly and respectfully so that she can feel safe and secure in your love and care again.

I would get close enough to make eye contact and tell her once politely not to do it ("please keep your toys in the house"), and then say, "You are throwing toys outside when I asked you not to. I'm going to lock the door." She may squawk in response, or even have a meltdown, but she will also breathe a huge inward sigh of relief. *Mommy stopped me before she got mad. She seems confident about taking care of me.*

Taking care of yourself and your child — prioritizing your relationship to this extent — is the ultimate in great parenting and something to feel extremely proud of. Children don't want to be considered bothersome, frustrating, or annoying, and they don't deserve our resentment. But only *we* can set the limits necessary (and early enough) to prevent these feelings from cropping up and poisoning our relationship.

I hope this perspective helps give you the encouragement you need to remain calm and be consistent.

Warmly,
Janet

24.

The Truth About Consequences

When navigating an area of parenting as tricky as discipline, it can help to routinely check in with ourselves with an important question: What are our ultimate parenting goals?

If our primary goal is an enduring bond with our kids, then repeated phrases like "make him understand," "drum this concept into his head," and even "*get* him to do such-in-such" are clear signs we've derailed.

Starting from a place of manipulation is not a good strategy. It will continually undermine us, because it creates an us-against-them relationship rather than the positive partnership kids need to be guided effectively.

Although consequences do play a meaningful role in respectful discipline (which I explain below), consequences don't work when:

They are just a euphemism for punishments. Punishments may sometimes succeed in deterring undesirable behavior, though more often than not parents discover that punishments lead to many more punishments. Punishments are inadequate teachers because they don't teach or model *positive* behavior.

They can also have unfortunate, unintended consequences. Punishments cause children to internalize shame and anger, create distance, isolation, and mistrust. Severe or physical punishments can create fear, rage, helplessness, and hopelessness.

Psychologist Paul Bloom's fascinating studies on babies and morals show that even young infants have a basic understanding of fairness. A respectful consequence will feel fair to our children. Which isn't to say they won't object to it — they probably will — and that disagreement needs to be accepted and acknowledged. When sincerity and fairness are sensed by our children, the trust between us remains intact and often even strengthens.

Punishments feel petty because they are. Is this the aspect of our personality we want our children to emulate?

They are unrelated to the situation and/or given too long after the fact. One of the many inspiring things children do is live in the moment. They've *so* moved on. And the younger the child, the sooner they've forgotten completely and can't make the connection between their action and our consequence. So when we set limits about anything with our kids, we need to do it immediately and move on, too, without brooding, seething, or grudges.

With a bit of forethought, we could have avoided or prevented the situation by creating a boundary or setting a limit. Older children need to be able to protect their projects (on a high table, for example) from infants and toddlers, who are all about exploring and testing. It's not fair to either child for parents to allow a destructive incident to happen if it is possible to prevent it.

They include forced apologies or other inauthentic gestures. Forcing apologies and forgiveness or any other feeling teaches children many unproductive things: Don't trust your true feelings, pretend to feel things to please adults, use "I'm sorry" as an excuse, be a phony, etc.

Consequences are effective, respectful, and relationship-building when they are:

1. Logical, reasonable, age-appropriate choices. "I can't let you throw those blocks toward the window... You are having a hard time not throwing the blocks. You can throw them toward the rug or in the basket, or I will need to put them away for now... Thank you for letting me know you need help. I'll put the blocks away."

2. Stated kindly and confidently (rather than as a threat), and then we let go and move on. For most of us, this means we must *set the limit early*, before we get too annoyed or angry.

3. Coupled with acknowledgement of our child's point-of-view and feelings (no matter how unreasonable they might seem). "You wanted to stay at the park, but you had a hard time not hitting your friends, so I said we had to go. I hear how upset you are."

4. Consistent, predictable responses, elements of

a routine that our child recognizes. "Are you finished eating? You are standing up and that tells me you're done... Okay, you're sitting back down for more, please don't get up until you're finished... Oh, now you're up again, so I will put the food away. Thanks for letting me know you are done. ...You're upset that I put the food away. You didn't want me to do that. I understand. We'll be eating again soon."

5. A genuine expression of our personal limits. Here's where I disagree with some of my fellow gentle discipline advocates...

A parent from one of my classes (who could not be a more respectful, caring, and all-around wonderful mom) attended a lecture by a popular, gentle parenting adviser. This mom's biggest challenge is setting limits confidently. She's especially prone to self-doubt and guilt if the situation pertains to her personal limits or isn't as clear-cut as a safety issue.

She asked the adviser about an experience she'd had while driving her six-year-old daughter to the home of a friend for a play date. Her daughter became upset with her toddler brother and would not stop screaming. The mom tried patiently asking her to stop several times, but she continued. The mom was at the end of her rope. She asked this adviser if it was okay for her to tell her daughter that if she couldn't stop yelling, they would be turning the car around and going back home. The adviser's answer was "no," because that was a parent-imposed consequence.

I'm not going to lie — hearing that drove me half-mad. Here is a mom who especially needs to be supported to set limits and stick up for herself, and instead she is scolded for suggesting it.

Ironically, this adviser specializes in helping parents stop yelling, and yet she misses a crucial piece of the yelling puzzle: parents need all the encouragement in the world to take care of themselves calmly, honestly, fairly, and confidently, so that they don't explode on their kids. They need permission to turn the car around, stop their children from taking out messy art supplies before they've helped clear up the previous ones, not go to the park when their child refuses to get dressed. "You said you wanted to go to the park today, but we won't have enough time unless you can get your clothes on. Shall I help you?" Or "I'm getting seriously tired, so please help me brush your teeth if you'd like a second book." Or "I see that you are very disappointed about missing the play date, but you wouldn't stop screaming, and I honestly couldn't take it anymore."

The essential difference between consequences and punishments is our sincere and honest sharing. We can't be gentle parents without taking care of our personal boundaries... and the consequences of that kind of modeling are all good.

25.

Letting Your Child Off the Hook

With my first child, learning to recognize and respond effectively to her tests and limit-pushing behavior (which seemed to spring out of nowhere towards the end of her first year) took a concerted effort.

A father I consulted with recently shared a spot-on analogy that helped me understand my personal struggle and connect some dots.

He and his wife had been sensitively handling their toddler's demands and clinginess, yet her behaviors were becoming more intense and frequent. I was recommending that they be more clear, direct, and unafraid of their child's strong feelings, and it suddenly clicked for him. "*Oh*, so this is like when someone wants to date you and you're not interested, but instead of being direct you try to let them down easy... and then they don't end up getting the message."

Bingo. That analogy really resonated, because that was once me. I avoided confrontation and saying "no". I didn't want to risk hurting anyone's feelings or make them angry at me. I did not want to be rejected, even when I was basically rejecting that person myself. I played it safe so I would continue to be "liked" and not create waves.

So, I made excuses and more excuses rather than simply admitting, "Thanks, but I'm not interested in dating you." Invariably, the guy would keep calling (no texting to hide behind back then, though I'm sure I would have appreciated it!), and I'd need to keep evading and avoiding him. I would become increasingly annoyed and resentful. *Can't he take a hint?* But whose fault was it? Mine, of course.

We can create a similar dynamic with our children. We string them along when we are not clear and direct, usually because we don't want to face the music. *Understandably.* Screaming, crying and tantrums aren't music to anyone's ears, but when we attempt to avoid or tiptoe around our children's feelings, their undesirable behavior and neediness usually continue (or crop up again later), and then we are the ones who end up screaming. We have only ourselves to blame.

The most loving way to say "no" is directly, confidently, and long before we become annoyed or angry. This isn't about being harsh, and it's definitely not punitive. It's simply being decisive — *projecting calm conviction.*

It is best to use the actual word "no" only occasionally, because children tune it out if we use it too much. It's also not as respectful or clarifying as "I won't let you, because that hurts," or "I can't let you, because that isn't safe," or "I can't play with you right now. I need to get our dinner ready."

However, when parents and children are having difficulties because the parents aren't being direct and clear enough, I do encourage them to say (or at least think in terms of) "no," along with a very brief explanation. "No" can help parents (and therefore children) feel more clear. Children will often let us know that they need even more clarity by continuing the limit-pushing behavior. They need to know we mean what we say and are comfortable following through and stopping them.

We can't be clear with our toddlers if we don't have clarity ourselves. This is why issues involving safety tend to be the easiest for parents to say "no" to. Much more challenging are less clear-cut issues like:

- Weaning
- Separations that aren't absolutely necessary (like we want to go to the bathroom or somewhere else in the house while leaving our child in a safe play area)
- Bedtime and sleep issues (even less clear because we're tired and our defenses our down)
- Our child's preference for one parent while with the other parent
- Stalling

Another parent I consulted with recently was struggling to get comfortable setting limits with her toddler, but she was able to help *me* help *her* when she told me about the one situation that had always felt crystal clear: Insisting her son hold hands in the parking lot.

Every time she brought up a situation in which she wavered (like when she needed him to finish his bath and sensed he was stalling), I'd remind her, "You're holding his hand in the parking lot." That's how clear we need to be. Remember, there's always the option of changing our mind (clearly) later.

Also remember that toddlers are incredibly aware, especially tuned in to their parents, and learning all the time. So the question is never "Are they learning?" It's "*What* are they learning?"

When we feel uneasy or unsure saying "no" in a particular situation, and perhaps we try to coax, cajole, make it work for our child, she has no choice but to feel uneasy.

If we worry about our child's feelings in response to our boundaries (perhaps we tread lightly or try to console our "poor baby"), she has no choice but to feel uncomfortable with these feelings.

When our kids sense us using kid gloves around them, they feel weak and incapable instead of healthy and willful like toddlers need to be, and they have no choice but to continue playing the role we've unwittingly chosen for them.

To make matters even murkier, while our children are getting messages from us through our every interaction, we are also getting input from them. So, our hesitancy to address guidance moments directly creates discomfort for our children, which they might express through clingy, needy behavior. Then (egads!) our fears are confirmed: We see a fragile, anxious, needy child whom we dare not disappoint. And the cycle continues.

So, parents are called to be brave and let their children off the hook by giving them direct responses. We must speak to our children's strengths rather than fearing their weaknesses. They deserve the truth. And they can handle it, but only if we believe they can.

26.

How to Be a Gentle Leader

The freedom we all feel deep within ourselves comes once we understand where we stand in the scheme of things.
                                                    – Magda Gerber

A frustrated, exhausted mom wants to treat her three-year-old more gently and less punitively. Ironically, the way to do that may be to become a stronger leader.

Janet,

I feel like I have failed as a parent.

I have a three-year-old daughter who on most days is difficult, to say the least. She screams, yells, hits, constantly interrupts, tantrums, tells us "no," throws toys, refuses to listen..... Then there are shining moments when she is well-behaved, listens and is wonderful, but it seems like they are few and far between.

I get frustrated. Very frustrated.

We also have an 8-month-old son who demands my attention, and my daughter hates it. She is always saying that I **have** *to take care of her first, then him. She loves her little brother until I need to give him attention.*

We have done time-out, toy taking, early bed time, spanking... Everything that is "normal" to me having come from an authoritarian home . . . but it doesn't work. Nothing works. The only thing that it does is make everyone involved feel like poo.

My house is chaos. My beautiful girl is not only miserable, but acts like she is scared of us because she hates punishment... Our son senses the tension and it causes issues with him. And I feel like a failure as a parent.

I know you are probably swamped with e-mails, but I hope that you get a chance to read this and possibly help enlighten an exhausted momma, because I just don't know what to do anymore.

Sincerely,
Kelly

Hi, Kelly:

Please forgive me to taking so long to respond. I have been slow responding to all my emails lately, but especially the ones that I don't have easy answers for (even though those are probably the people who need responding to most!).

And while I'm apologizing... I'm also sorry for all you are going through, that you are doubting yourself and getting discouraged.

It's admittedly challenging for me to dive in and understand a family's dynamics from the scant information in an email. So when I read, I look for clues, and then I try to figure out why those things stand out. In your letter it was this: *"She is always saying that I **have** to take care of her first, then him."*

That statement, along with her being "miserable," and the fact that she "screams, yells, hits, and so on," indicates to me that the balance of power between you and your daughter might not be as healthy as it could be. She seems to be under the impression that she can exert control in areas that aren't hers to lead. She sounds unsettled and uncomfortable, and your responses, interventions, and disciplinary measures seem to be unsettling her even more rather than easing her mind, addressing her need to test her power, and helping her to feel safe, nested, more comfortable, and free.

So, how can we help?

I would start by echoing Magda's admonition that children need gentle leaders. They need to know without a doubt that their parents are in charge. This may seem obvious, but it's easy to get a little confused in this area, especially with a strong, bright, and verbal child. (I've been there.)

Sometimes a reticence to set clear boundaries stems from being raised in an overly strict home. Perhaps there is a fear of being too authoritative and repeating patterns of response that our parents modeled — responses that felt unloving, disconnecting, or even abusive. Or, sometimes, the parent is simply inexperienced at establishing healthy boundaries.

But when we don't make it clear that we are the loving leaders of the house by setting reasonable, consistent limits and taking control, our child has no choice but to feel *out of control*.

Believe it or not, your daughter isn't comfortable being in the position of saying, "You *have* to take care of me first" (which is very different from saying, "I want you to take care of me first!"). She doesn't want the power that implies. It makes her feel unsafe and uneasy to be three years old and making those kinds of statements, but this isn't something she's consciously aware of, so it's difficult for us to see, too.

This out-of-control feeling leads to more out-of-control behavior, hence the screams, yells, hits, etc., which then make parents feel out of control. Rather than leading confidently, we might react out of anger, frustration, and desperation. We might resort to trying to regain control through punishments like spankings and disciplinary tactics like time-out that result in even more rebellion and disconnectedness. This makes us feel like failures.

Family life is easier and less chaotic for everyone when we are all clear about our roles. So, how do we do that?

1. Set limits calmly, firmly, gently, and *early*. By setting limits early, I mean making situations as clear as possible for your daughter before she even begins to act out. This clarity helps parents, too, because those well-defined boundaries keep us feeling on top of the situation and prevent us from reaching our wit's end — getting frustrated and angry and resorting to punishments.

Here's an example: you say to your daughter, "I'm getting ready to feed the baby and put him to bed. I'll be busy with him for the next half hour. If you need something, I can get it now."

Then, after getting her what she needs (a book from the shelf, a snack, whatever), give her a choice. "You can sit in the room with us very quietly or go to your room and play." You might even ask, "What will you do in your room while I'm busy?"

Let's say she chooses staying with you quietly but doesn't end up being able to manage it, and she's whiny. "I know it's hard to wait while I'm busy with the baby, but I need your help. I want you to go to your room and play or look at books until we're finished. Then I'll have time to be with you."

Then let's say she tries to hit you. You hold her hand. "I won't let you hurt me. I see you're upset. You can go to your room and hit your pillows, but I won't let you hit me."

As strong as your daughter sounds, I imagine she has (and will continue to have) intense negative reactions when you set limits. Don't be uncomfortable with that. View the yelling, screaming, and crying as healthy and positive releases for her. It's hard being a toddler and *really* hard also being a big sister and having to share your parents with someone small, adorable, and needy. Acknowledge her feelings whenever possible: "I know it's hard for you when I'm busy with the baby. It's so hard and upsetting to have to wait, but I know you can do it."

Try to relax – or, at least, *seem* relaxed — and maintain composure even if she's exploding. Eventually, when she knows you mean what you say and she's unable to rattle you, she'll settle into a routine of occupying herself when you are busy with the baby.

I went through something similar with my intense and assertive eldest daughter after my second baby was born. She was four years old and would complain, cry, scream, and howl when I needed time to feed her sister and put her to bed, which used to take me a whole hour. It was a scene for several days. Finally, she discovered on her own that she could spend that time playing in her room with her dollhouse, and that became her self-chosen routine while I was focusing on her sister. I've no doubt that a lot of wild things happened in that dollhouse!

2. Acknowledge her point-of-view, but don't argue it. When your daughter expresses her disagreement with the situation, especially if her statement begins with "you have to," acknowledge it calmly, look beyond it to what she's feeling when there's time, but don't argue ("No, I *don't* have to."), negotiate, or otherwise give it power. Your short answer might be something along the lines of a sincere "Thank you for your opinion. Here's the plan..."

A longer response might delve deeper into acknowledging her feelings, which with a new sibling can include anger and grief over the loss of the one-on-one relationship with the parent. Still, make it clear that you hear her feelings, but that you are making the plan. She needs your empathy, but not the kind of "poor baby" sympathy that makes us go soft on behavior limits. In fact, for a child in transition, consistent, firm boundaries are even more vital.

3. Ask her to help. Help fulfill her healthy needs for autonomy, competence, and participation by asking for her assistance with the baby (and anything else) whenever possible.

4. Give reassurance, one-on-one attention, and gratitude. Assure her that her needs will always be met, even though it won't always be in her perfect time. And don't forget to provide periods of undivided attention that she can look forward to regularly. Most importantly, don't forget to thank her for the "*shining moments when she is well-behaved, listens and is wonderful.*"

Hopefully, these suggestions will help your daughter understand that her opinions and feelings are always welcome and understood, but family decisions (like whose needs are being met when) will always be made by you, no matter how much she objects. This should help ease her mind and at least some of the chaos you're dealing with.

Please keep me posted!

Warmly,

Janet

27.

If Gentle Discipline Isn't Working

If you're reading this book because you're committed to guiding your child's behavior without spankings or punishments, I salute you — especially if you were punished as a child and are looking for a better way.

Setting limits without punishments works. In fact, it works so beautifully that you'll find you need to set fewer and fewer limits, especially once the toddler years have passed. This is not hyperbole. I receive hundreds of emails every year from elated parents who share their success stories.

I also hear a lot about what *isn't* working from parents who believe they are practicing gentle discipline. Parents share about behavior that might have started as minor testing but has become more aggressive, destructive, defiant, or deliberate. I hear about needy, demanding five-year-olds, preschoolers intentionally hurting their peers, and children who seem either fragile or angry much of the time.

Parents wonder: *How can my child keep acting this way when I'm committed to respectful, non-punitive guidance?*

I had a sudden inkling about the reason while re-reading blogger Suchada Eickemeyer's article: "The

Most Valuable Parenting Phrase After 'I Love You'." The key phrase she refers to is "I won't let you." Suchada remarks, "This phrase has helped me become the disciplinarian I want to be: in charge, but not controlling; gentle, but firm; honest; clear; and direct."

There seems to be a common misconception that gentle, non-punitive discipline means avoiding a direct confrontation with the child rather than providing the simple, connected response children need when, for example, they hit the dog. In this case, appropriate discipline would mean getting down on the floor next to the child, making eye contact, and saying calmly, "I won't let you hit the dog. That hurts," while holding the child's hand or otherwise blocking another hit.

My sense is that many parents over-complicate this issue, perhaps because of confusion about some of the terms commonly used in regard to discipline; terms like 'connection', 'unmet needs', and 'playful'.

Connection

Yes, children need to feel connected for discipline to be successful. But how? When I hear the word 'connection', hugging, laughing and running through grass together come to mind, not saying "no" and possibly upsetting my child. Connection during boundary setting doesn't look warm and fuzzy, but it is crucial. Here are the two most important ways to connect:

1. **Just talk to your child.** Most of the advice I hear about setting limits suggests wording that subtly skirts a direct confrontation and distances us when we should be connecting. The verbal examples are

commonly in third person: "It is not okay to..."; "Mommy doesn't like it when you..."; or "Joey isn't allowed to..."

Then there's the philosophical approach: "Faces are not for slapping"; "Streets are not for running into"; "Friends are not for biting."

Or, the 'royal we': "We don't throw food" (while our perceptive toddlers are thinking: *Well, some of us don't*).

Personally, I'm even a little uncomfortable with "Honey (or Sweetie, or Pumpkin), don't hurt the dog." Terms of endearment at times like these sound phony and patronizing to me, especially if the adult is feeling annoyed while faking calm and affection.

"I won't let you" (or "I can't let you" or "I don't want you to") instantly connect us person-to-person and clarify our expectations. This is the connection children need first and foremost when they misbehave. Toddlers don't miss a trick, so they need (and deserve) a respectful, straight answer. We can run through the grass together afterwards.

2. Acknowledge and empathize. Children need their perspective and feelings acknowledged when we are setting limits. It is usually best to empathize after first setting the limit ("I won't let you"). But empathy means understanding and supporting, not going down with the ship. In other words, reflect verbally ("You were upset about not getting another cracker."), but don't get upset or discouraged when your child has an emotional reaction to your limits. That level of connection isn't healthy for either of us. It wears us out and clouds our perspective, making effective guidance less possible, and our child is without the strong anchor she needs.

Unmet Needs

By the time they are 18 months of age, most children are fully aware of many of the things we don't want them to do. So, why do they do them? There are many possibilities to consider, but only *after* we fulfill the child's number one need in that moment of limit-pushing behavior. If we hesitate to set a limit with conviction because we're trying to figure out what is driving our child's behavior, he or she is left with a faltering, vague, or inconclusive message instead of real help.

The most common need children have when they act out is our attention, beginning with a very specific kind of attention — a kind but firm acknowledgement of their behavior and of our expectation.

Playful

Anyone who knows me can tell you that I'm a silly, playful person and parent. I love the genuine, spontaneous playfulness and joking that happens with children when I feel confident about my leadership. Playfulness is wonderful when we're "feeling it," and it helps us encourage cooperation for cleaning up toys or brushing teeth. But I don't advise playfulness as a technique for limit setting when it replaces (or dances around) the connected, honest, clear response children need.

I also think advising playfulness imposes even more pressure on parents to keep children happy all the time, which most of us would do if we thought it possible, or healthy, or the route to true happiness. But always smiling isn't real life or a real relationship. Our kids know better, and they deserve both.

28.

Parenting a Strong-Willed Child

After years of observing young children, teaching parents, and being somewhat conscious of my own learning process, I've become increasingly fascinated by the way we humans learn. I find it especially ironic that we can be presented with helpful information or ideas, even repeatedly, yet for whatever reason they don't resonate enough with us to put them into practice. But then we come across that same content in slightly different wrapping, in a new circumstance, or at a later time, and suddenly it hits us like a revelation.

Juliet is an engaging, loving mom I've conferenced with a few times. She allowed me to share this personal note describing a transformative moment she experienced regarding "gentle leadership" and her strong-willed daughter, Cleo:

For the last four months or so I was feeling pretty exhausted and was struggling. Cleo is, as you know, an incredibly strong kid. So strong that I rarely see her on the losing end of a toy struggle, even with older kids. She is both physically and willfully strong.

I admire this in her so much and feel very protective of it, because as a child I learned to put aside my strength in favor of making sure that everyone around me was comfortable and happy. It has taken me years to learn to stand my ground and not be so overly concerned about everyone else. Of course, I get a daughter who makes me learn it even more deeply!

As Cleo has gotten older (two in July), her determination and willfulness have only increased, and although I thought I was being firm, I really wasn't. I never waffled on limits, but I did steel myself for her reaction in a way that wasn't helpful. Sometimes when I had to physically carry her when she didn't want to be carried, she could make it so difficult that I had to use all of my strength and resources to do it in a way that was both effective and gentle. I noticed that I was feeling beaten down by her responses and sometimes resentfully thinking to myself, "Jeez, kid, can't you be a little easier?!"

What I recognize now is that she was feeling all of this (my weakening resolve) and probably felt too powerful, concerned that mama wasn't strong enough to handle her, and was likely getting the unsettling message that she was too much.

After reading your article about timers (Chapter 11), I had an internal shift, and things changed completely. I recognized that I am strong enough to handle her reactions and don't have to take them on... I can be a sounding board for her and gently and firmly follow through and guide her where she needs to go. With this change in perception, I no longer feel exhausted at the end of the day and feel the happiness as a mom I have rarely known — save for the past few months.

The funny thing is that this is all internal. On the outside my actions look largely the same, but the internal shift has made it so much easier for Cleo to cooperate with me and for me to be really present for her.

Cleo seems happier, too, with less need to test boundaries. In my own life, I know that around this age is when I suffered a lot of developmental trauma around losing agency and learning to fear my mom, who couldn't handle

141

my power. So to be navigating this time with Cleo in a way that feels so authentically respectful to me and to her is the greatest gift I can imagine.

Parenting in such an awake way is all about losing your way and finding it again. Thank you for your guidance.

Best,

Juliet

29.

When Respect Becomes Indulgence

Dear Janet,

As a developmental psychologist and professor, I love your website and blog. You do a great job explaining an approach to child development that is accepted by many in the academic community (at least in my area of research).

One issue that has been on my mind lately is how to determine what appropriate expectations are for a child of a given age. My son is approaching toddlerhood, and I want to try to prepare myself for what is to come. So how do you decide what is an appropriate expectation for a child of a given age?

For instance, recently we had some friends over with their 3-year-old. On their way out, she decided that she wanted to wear her mom's shoes to walk out to the car, which meant that it would take a lot longer and she might trip. What would be an appropriate response in that situation?

In another recent outing, a friend's toddler started banging his head against the floor, throwing a tantrum. What should she have done in response?

Thank you,
Michelle

Hi, Michelle:
Thank you for your note and questions. You

definitely got me thinking. At first, the only commonality I could see between the two examples you gave me was the need for a calm parent. "Appropriate expectations" threw me off a bit until I realized you were asking about appropriate *behavior*, which is a little different.

How do we know what to allow and where to draw the line? What are our children's true needs? Here are some general guidelines I put together using your examples.

Say YES

Say yes to feelings. Always. Children need freedom to express their deepest, darkest, oddest, most outrageous or inappropriate-seeming feelings.

Emotions are deeply connected to "self," so from infancy onwards our children need to know we will patiently hear and accept all their feelings and try our best to understand them. The challenge is not to squelch the feelings (with distractions, punishments, or other invalidating responses), and also not to let the emotional outbursts impact us too much — to hear and support our child without absorbing her moods.

I've found it helpful to remind myself that we can't control another person's feelings. We can only control the freedom our child feels to express them. Encouraging the expression of feelings and acknowledging them is the key to our child's emotional health and also to self-worth.

Toddlers have tantrums because they reach a tipping point and need to release intense emotions that are way beyond their control. The child who falls to the floor and bangs his head in anger, rage, or frustration needs a calm, understanding parent to allow him to express these feelings fully — not punish him, or even "comfort" him, to make this outburst stop.

The tantrum has to run its course to be an effective release for the child. Then we acknowledge the situation and offer hugs. "Wow, you were so upset that I said you couldn't have another piece of that yummy cake. You really wanted more."

If head-banging becomes a frequent habit, definitely consult a professional, but the typical child will not deliberately hurt himself. A calm, accepting attitude, while perhaps slipping a pillow under the child's head ("I'm putting this here to keep you safe"), is our best response.

If we become frantic, punitive, or agitated (in other words, we let the behavior push our buttons), the child might consciously repeat it.

Say yes to safe exploration, self-directed play. For young children, play, exploration, and experimentation should be predominantly self-chosen. Our children's choices will surprise us and not always look like play as we might perceive it. Facilitating and observing self-directed play is one of the biggest joys of caring for babies and toddlers. And for our children, this freedom is an essential need (*and* it helps them accept our boundaries more readily). Ideally, we provide the opportunities and materials and let children take it from there.

I see no problem at all with allowing children to play in mom's shoes if mom doesn't mind. But, as I'll explain below, our child's need to explore doesn't mean she needs to do this anywhere besides the places we deem safe or appropriate.

Give Boundaries

Give boundaries for safety. This means keeping an eye on the head banging, which is probably an involuntary, temporary phase (and if we can stay calm, will probably stay that way).

Wearing mom's shoes to the car is a risk that is not necessary for healthy experimentation. The true wish or "need" this child is expressing, in my opinion, is the comfort of a parent's leadership and limits.

Give boundaries when the child is testing. I see the request to go to the car in mom's shoes as a test of wills, and if she wins, she loses. Secretly, I think she's hoping mom will care enough to say no. She sounds like a strong, bright girl, probably very capable of making it to the car in high heels if she were allowed to. But then there would probably be another test.

Rather than engage in battles, I advise rising above them by calmly and lovingly setting a limit: "I know you like to walk in my shoes, and that's safe to do in our house, but not now. Would you like to wear your shoes or go barefoot?" She'll either accept this gracefully or object and release some of the feelings that have been simmering inside her.

Give boundaries during transitions. Young children tend to have difficulty with transitions, which means they usually need the comfort of more direction and less choice than they do at play time. They still need opportunities for autonomy, like choosing whether or not to wear *their* shoes to the car (if that's an option) or the choice, "Would you like to walk or be carried?" But the freedom to make everyone wait while they explore walking "as Mommy does" is indulging them with an uncomfortable amount of power.

The Annoyance Factor

Parenting is the development of an extremely vital relationship, the model for every future relationship our child will engage in. Since a relationship takes two, our needs and feelings are just as important as our child's. Yes, we make many sacrifices as parents, but ultimately, the relationship has to work for both of us.

Since we are the adults in charge, we are the only ones capable of protecting our relationship from being one of resentment, dishonesty, distrust, dislike. This is why I believe in giving boundaries to prevent the *annoyance factor*. Meaning, whenever possible, we don't give children the freedom to irritate us through their behavior. (Yes, expressions of emotion can be very annoying, but those don't count, because we cannot and should not control them.)

If we don't want our daughter playing with our shoes, I don't believe we should allow it, and instead of feeling guilty we should feel good about taking care of ourselves and prioritizing our relationship.

We make it even easier for our child not to irritate us by making off-limit items unavailable to her while she plays. This is one of the many reasons safe, enclosed play spaces are invaluable. They give children the freedom to fulfill their healthy, instinctual need to explore without being a nuisance to us, and hearing a "no" (that they are inclined not to obey) every few minutes. It's a baby's job to get into everything, and when we constantly have to say, "Stop that," and "Stay out of there," we start to feel resentful.

Also, when we placate children by allowing them to do what we don't *really* want them to do, we end up being the ones who want to explode, and that can be dangerous.

Do we want our children to grow up believing they are annoying, unpleasant people... and very possibly fulfilling that prophecy?

It helps to be strongly attuned to our own inner-rhythm – to know what your needs are, and to convey this to your family so they learn to respect your needs, too. Ongoingly sacrificing your own needs for the child's can create inward anger within both of you."

– Magda Gerber, *Dear Parent: Caring for Infants With Respect*

I hope this sheds some light.
Warmly,
Janet

30.

Guilt-Free Discipline (A Success Story)

Parents are often reluctant to set limits for children because they'd rather not face the push-back and negative reactions (can't imagine why). We don't feel good when our kids are unhappy, and it feels even worse when we're responsible for it. We might feel guilty, worrying that our children's disappointment or anger will linger, or fearing they will feel unloved or stop loving us because we didn't let them do what they wanted.

Nothing could be further from the truth.

Providing boundaries with honesty and respect is the surest way to foster emotional security, which will endow our children with a lifetime of happiness and freedom.

I am always thrilled to receive positive feedback from readers that demonstrates RIE principles in action. In this email from Stephanie, she shares an experience that brilliantly illustrates three essential ingredients for successful, respectful discipline:

1. Respectful communication. We intervene with even our youngest infants directly and honestly rather than resorting to distraction, tricks, coaxing, or other types of disconnected, dishonest responses and manipulation.

2. Setting limits early. We register our annoyance before it turns to frustration or anger, and we realize this is a sign that we need to set a limit. Since we know it's patently unfair to allow our negative feelings to infringe upon our relationship with our child, we perceive these limits as positive and loving.

3. Following through. We recognize that our verbal directions and requests are often not enough, even when our children fully understand them. So we assure children that we will "help" them by confidently following through with gentle but insistent actions.

Stephanie's Story

I wanted to write and tell you about an interaction with my 2-year-old daughter last night. I had come home from work, and while I was talking with my husband she began to dump the clean clothes from the laundry basket onto the floor. At first I was not going to set a boundary because it was not really a safety issue, but then I felt myself getting annoyed, so I decided that it would be better to go ahead and stop her from dragging clean clothes over the dirt on the floor.

I crouched down to her level and said, "I won't let you drag the clothes across the floor. I don't want to have to wash them again." I gently removed the clothes from her hands, and she tried one more time to grab them from me. I softly deflected her hands and said, "I won't let you take them from me. I am putting them away." She cried for about 10 seconds then went on to play with her kitchen set.

As much as I believe in respectful parenting, for some reason it still amazes me when I have an interaction like that. The communication just seems so effortless and authentic, and I love the peace it brings to my home.

A short while later — and this is the best part — Genevieve came in close to me and gave me a hug. Then she said the most heartwarming thing to me...."I am so happy. I am so happy, Mama." And she meant it!

Boundaries help our children to feel safe and happy. Thank you for all your help in guiding parents to set them with love.

Many thanks to Stephanie and Genevieve for allowing me to share your inspiring experience!

31.

Respectful Parenting Is Not Passive Parenting

One of the most commonly misunderstood aspects of parenting is also the most critical: providing children the boundaries they need to feel secure.

I was reminded (again) how confusing this issue can be for all of us when I received this email from a reader about an article discussing hitting:

Like so many others, I am struggling with this issue daily. I feel somewhat validated knowing that my matter-of-fact response is on the right track. It can be difficult to remain visibly unruffled when grandma or another observer is present and yelling, "Don't hit your mother like that!"

One thing that continues to be an issue for me is the "I won't let you..." approach. My toddler son is big for his age and quite strong. Trying to restrain his hands or feet is difficult for a petite woman like me. It's even more difficult when I try the approach you mentioned: "Can you come inside by yourself, or do you need my help?"

If the kicking, hitting, and biting starts when you try to pick up the child, but you can't just walk away, what's next?

- Sara

Unruffled, calm, and *matter-of-fact* are words I often use to help parents understand that intense responses to their kids' behavior tend to backfire. Our children need to know that their parents and caregivers are not thrown by their minor misdeeds, so they can rest assured that they are well taken care of and not more powerful than the leaders they depend on.

A two or three-year-old whose normal, healthy boundary testing causes fear or anger in an adult can't feel safe.

So, Sara's comment was a little perplexing to me until I realized that unruffled and matter-of-fact (and even respect) can easily be misconstrued as being passive rather than confidently in charge. This reminded me that passivity is one of the most common discipline FAILS I see.

Here's what I wrote back:

Sara:

If my kids' grandma yelled, "Don't hit your mother like that!," I would be agreeing, "Yeah, don't hit your mother! I'm not going to let you do that." This reaction would not come from a place of anger. It would be firm and out of assurance that I am helping my child. Do you think you might be confusing unruffled and matter-of-fact with *passive* or *timid*? It sounds like your son needs much more assurance and confident leadership from you.

You say your boy is quite strong, but you are stronger, aren't you? It can be disconcerting and even frightening for young children to feel like their parents can't physically contain them.

It's hard for me to know exactly how to advise you with just the information you've given me, but your boy's behavior indicates that he is not getting the helpful, comforting, firm responses he needs.

I would also make sure you are preparing him in advance for transitions and speaking to him honestly and respectfully.

There are two extreme approaches to discipline that do not serve a toddler's needs. One is overly strict, punitive, and non-empathetic. It involves maintaining control of the household through punitive discipline and other manipulative tactics. The child is perceived as innately "bad" and out-of-control, needing to be taught how to behave through fear and shame. Respect is *demanded* from children rather than being something children can be trusted to return to us when they have been treated respectfully from the time they are born.

On the other end of the spectrum are parents who are reticent to engage in conflict and will do almost anything to avoid their child's disagreement. These parents hope boundaries will be accepted by their toddler, so they set limits timidly, softly, perhaps with a wavering tone that asks *is this going to be okay with you?*

Perhaps they over-identify with their child's feelings, so their instinct is to go out of their way to "make it work" in order to keep the child happy. The parent's thought might be *why not avoid an emotional outburst whenever possible?* The parent rationalizes: *I wanted to go to the bathroom alone this time, but I didn't really need to;* or *it's probably okay for us to be late while I wait for Alice to decide she's ready to get into her car seat. I can't force her.*

There is a lack of recognition of the healthy need toddlers have to express their burgeoning will by resisting *whatever* their parents want, as well as their need to release intense feelings.

These parents might worry that their child's spirit will be crushed, or she'll stop loving or trusting them if there is a conflict of will. They coax or distract their child into the behavior they want (or out of the behavior they don't want) rather than risk being the mean guy who says "no".

"Basically, most parents are afraid of disciplining their children because they are afraid of the power struggle. They are afraid of overpowering the child, afraid they will destroy the child's free will and personality. This is an erroneous attitude."

– Magda Gerber

Passive parents often give too many choices, overanalyze, or respond ambiguously when children need a definitive, honest intervention. In the extreme, when a child hits a peer, her parent might ask her, "Was that a good choice?" Hard to believe, but I know someone who witnessed this.

Every tear a child sheds goes straight to the sensitive parent's heart. But no matter how caring these parents are, the child's testing continues. It must, because the child is still not getting the help she needs.

"There is no way over-indulged children are going to be happy, because they seldom get direct, honest responses from their parents. ...When you say "no," really mean it. Let your face and posture reflect "no" as well."

– Magda Gerber

These children might seem adrift and

uncomfortable much of the time. There may be a lot of demanding, crying, and whining rather than healthy coping and resilience, which can send even the kindest, gentlest, most loving parents over the edge. "How could our child keep pushing us when we are so loving, kind and respectful?" But the child's behavior is not *in spite of* the parent's efforts to please, or their gentle, peaceful attitude. It is *because* of it.

If this passive approach continues, these children can become unpleasant company, not only for their parents, but for their peers, teachers, family, and friends.

"A positive goal to strive for when disciplining would be to raise children we not only love, but in whose company we love being."

– Magda Gerber

Guess which of these two discipline approaches I have more experience helping parents with?

That might be because "follow the child" philosophies like RIE can confuse parents about their role. Parents are encouraged to respect their babies, trust them to develop skills naturally according to their inborn timetable, and lead play.

As facilitators of these aspects of our child's development rather than teachers, we learn to observe. We practice staying out of the way. But this must not be confused with passivity. It is *mindfulness*.

32.

Gentle Discipline in Action

"Distracting and redirecting did not fool him. Time-outs and rewards did not motivate him."

This is the story of a bright, spirited toddler with exceptionally loving parents who felt their family "spiraling out of control." All they really needed were some simple tools to help them understand how to communicate with their son as a whole person and set limits with respect.

These are the practices that turned everything around for this family:

1. Respectful, honest, first-person communication.

2. Acknowledging desires and feelings.

3. Keeping directions simple and concise.

4. A confident, matter-of-fact, unquestioning tone.

5. Gently following through. For example, catching the child's hands (or feet) when he lashes out while saying, "I won't let you hit." If we don't follow through, children stop taking our directions seriously.

6. Limiting screens and over-stimulating toys.

7. Belief in their child's ability to actively participate in creating solutions.

This is the letter I received from Christine, which is wonderfully specific, intuitive, and entirely gratifying:

Dear Janet,

I came across your blog ten days ago and it has clearly and truly changed my life. A Facebook friend shared your article "What Your Toddler Thinks of Discipline" and it hit me like a brick wall. I spent the next two days reading your work — as much as I could, whenever I could. I think I made it all the way back to articles from 2010.

My son Nicky is 2.75 years old. All of his life he's been a late bloomer. He does everything normally, but it tends to happen 30% later than other children. We took him to doctors and specialists, and everything is healthy. He's just operating on his own timetable.

He's always had a very strong and fiery temperament, a gift and curse inherited from me. Since his speech hasn't developed on time, he started developing ways to let out the frustration at being constantly misunderstood or even, I'm sorry to say, ignored. It was a vicious cycle. The more his frustrations were unacknowledged, the worse his behavior would get. The worse his behavior became, the more punitive I became, and the more permissive his father became.

Two weeks ago my husband and I were crying at our kitchen table, unhappy with who we'd become and the way it felt like our family was spiraling out of control.

I had looked for help before, but nothing seemed to fit.

Distracting and redirecting did not fool him. Time-outs and rewards did not motivate him. Most of the advice I found for kids his age assumed a language skill he does not yet have. All of the advice I found for handling language delays was written for special needs children. Finding your blog and RIE was such a relief.

Finally, a way to communicate with the whole person inside my pre-verbal child.

When I read your blog, the first thing that I realized was how confusing the language I used with him could be. I framed everything as a question and talked in third person. I would say things like, "There's no hitting, okay?" or "Mama said jumping-on- the-couch time is over." I was genuinely surprised when my son cooperated if I simply told him, "I'm not going to let you do that," or "I'm taking this away now."

I saw the results from just this one change, and I was sold. I began to acknowledge his desires and to speak in first person. I began to give names to the negative emotions he was feeling. I started to catch his hands or feet when he tried to hit, punch, throw, and shove, telling him gently, "I'm not going to let you do that." I began to sit closely and mostly silently when he would scream at the top of his lungs and just be present and available with his anger. I went through the house and removed two dozen batteries from the toys he has been gifted recently. He has never watched TV, but I stopped handing him the iPad to play with.

It's only been ten days, and yet it already feels like a lifetime ago that my husband and I were crying at the kitchen table. Our son is less angry and more cooperative. He is happier and more engaged with the world around him. He's even speaking more, telling me now, "Understand," when he comprehends things and, "Sad," when he's upset.

My husband saw the happier family he was coming home to and asked me to teach him what I've learned. He's no longer afraid of our son's big emotions and has learned to set limits while still acknowledging Nicky's feelings.

I think the defining moment of your methods working for us happened on Friday night. I was using my laptop and Nicky wanted to sit in my lap. As usual, he began kicking my laptop. Using what I learned, I caught his foot before he made contact. I told him, "You want to kick my laptop but I'm not going to let you do that. I know it's upsetting when you want to do something and I won't let you."

We went through this a couple of times, then Nicky retracted his foot, extended it again slowly, and then hovered it over my laptop and said, "Airplane." He waved his foot back and forth without kicking and continued to tell me, "Airplane, airplane." I smiled and talked to him about his airplane flying over the computer. I could hardly believe how peacefully the situation had resolved.

Since then, he has used this tactic for items that he is not allowed to touch, flying his "airplane" hands and feet near, exploring the item without touching it. I could not be more proud of his creative problem solving.

Janet, your writing has done more than change my life. It's given me my family back. We're now enjoying our son instead of counting the hours until bedtime. I know there's still plenty more work on this journey, but I am excited and full of hope.

- Christine

Thanks

To Magda Gerber, for transforming my life with your wisdom and spirit. And to Magda's children, Mayo, Daisy, and Bence, for continuing to honor me with your tremendous support.

To Lisa Sunbury (*RegardingBaby.org*), who remains my online "other half" and co-pioneer.

To all my associates, fellow bloggers, and ECE enthusiasts in the online world. Together, we are making a difference.

To the families in my classes, for your trust, inspiration, and encouragement. I learn more from you than you do from me.

To the readers who graciously allowed me to share their stories and letters. You always brighten my day.

To Mike, my devoted editor, publisher, co-parent, and so much more.

And to Charlotte, Madeline, and Ben, for making my heart soar with pride and gratitude. Thank you for teaching me what life is about and for making RIE and me look incredibly good.

Recommended Reading

Your Self-Confident Baby, Magda Gerber, Allison Johnson. Published by John Wiley & Sons, Inc. (1998)

Dear Parent: Caring for Infants With Respect, Magda Gerber. Published by Resources for Infant Educarers (2002)

No-Drama Discipline, Daniel J. Siegel, M.D. & Tina Payne Bryson, PhD. Published by Bantam (2014)

1,2,3...The Toddler Years, Irene Van der Zande. Published by Santa Cruz Toddler Care Center (1986)

Siblings Without Rivalry, Adele Faber & Elaine Mazlish. Published by W.W. Norton & Co (2012)

The Emotional Life of the Toddler, Alicia F. Lieberman, Ph.D.. Published by The Free Press (1995)

How To Talk So Kids Will Listen & Listen So Kids Will Talk, Adele Faber & Elaine Mazlish, Published by Avon Books (1980)

Infants, Toddlers, and Caregivers, Janet Gonzalez-Mena, Dianne Widmeyer Eyer. Published by Mayfield Publishing Company (1997)

Raising Your Spirited Child, Mary Sheedy Kurcinka, Published by HarperCollins (2012)

Say What You See For Parents and Teachers, Sandra R. Blackard. Published by Language of Listening (2012)

On the web:
RegardingBaby.org
MagdaGerber.org
TeacherTomsBlog.blogspot.com

CPSIA information can be obtained
at www.ICGtesting.com
Printed in the USA
FSHW02n0624130918
52263FS